unlock the fountain of untapped
courage and motivation
within you

Life
Beyond
Fears

unlock the fountain of untapped
courage and motivation
within you

Life Beyond Fears

By

PEYUSH BHATIA

Published Internationally by

Pendown Press
Powered by Gullybaba

PENDOWN PRESS

Powered by **Gullybaba Publishing House Pvt. Ltd.,**
An ISO 9001 & ISO 14001 Certified Co.,
Regd. Office: 2525/193, 1st Floor, Onkar Nagar-A, Tri Nagar,
Delhi-110035
Ph.: 09350849407, 09312235086
E-mail: info@pendownpress.com
Branch Office: 1A/2A, 20, Hari Sadan, Ansari Road,
Daryaganj, New Delhi-110002
Ph.: 011-45794768
Website: PendownPress.com

First Edition: 2020
Price:
ISBN: 978-93-90479-13-9

Dedicated to...
My parents who made me fearless
& always inspired me to follow my dreams,
no matter what.

I owe you my ability to love, break through
my barriers, accept myself just as I am,
and create my own reality.

Contents

Preface

I was unaware of the devastating effect of fear till the time I found myself at its receiving end. It had engulfed me to the extent that my life came at a standstill. I am brutally frank to admit that as my own progress stopped, I started becoming jealous of the people around me. I had become the prisoner of the jailor called FEAR. All that I could do was to submit myself and accept its dominance. I had become the puppet of its hands. It was dictating my life, throwing my life out of gear, and the deluge of despondency had dogged my steps.

One day, it so happened (I have mentioned the incident in detail in this book) that I felt: I can ill afford to allow these things any more. I will have to be either brave or ready myself to be buried. If there is no life in life, it is not worth living for the sake of living. And that Spark, I will say, was the genesis of my transformation. When I refused to live the way I was living for so long, some good things started happening. Brewing negative thoughts lessened and encouraging and positive thoughts started making their way into my mind. When I took hold of myself, I started controlling certain things and its impact was favourable. These silver linings in my cloudy conditions gave me a fillip to think in that direction, prepare my check list, work on my grey areas and do my damndest to wriggle out of the (troubled) situation.

As soon as I started reaping benefits of my decision (not to be the victim of Fear), my mental preparation, my interaction with the people, whom I thought will be helpful, and my involvement in the work that I love to do got intensified. I had immersed myself in the ocean of Life Beyond Fear, hoping against hope, that I will one day find the pearls (the days of tranquility). I kept on trying with faith and the visualization that I will be leading a life of normalcy.

So many things happened in between, and finally the day of epiphany arrived. I became certain of creating my life asked I was certain to write my name whenever I am asked. My confidence soared. I was no longer hoping or wishing for those things, for I knew these are already mine. I could feel the aura of abundance around me. And, by the grace of God, I achieved what I had longed for.

After getting the prized possession of my life, I started toying with the idea of serving my society as there are hundreds of thousands of people across the globe, suffering from the deleterious effects of fear. The loss is immeasurable, so no person should be left in the lurch. With that thought, I was determined to write a book. I have put all the things that are worth knowing for a person reeling under the pressure and shock of fear. I hope, this book will immensely help people like me.

Acknowledgements

This book would not have been possible without the generosity of the Universe and the people around me. I would like to acknowledge and thank my Gurus, teachers, family, and friends for their constant guidance and unconditional support, through the journey of writing this book and always.

My Story Of Transformation

Today, as I write this book, I am living a peaceful and successful life and have established myself as a life coach. But it was not always like this.

I would like to pay my gratitude to the Universe and everyone around me to bring me out of the dark and help me achieve whatever I could. Thank you, Universe, for keeping me to alive and making me the trustee of this wisdom; for enabling me to share it with other people and become a medium for their transformation and self-healing.

I feel extremely blessed to contribute to the divine cause of healing this Universe and raising its vibration to a higher level, transforming it from negative to positive.

Are you thinking, "what is she talking about?"

Yes, I am grateful. I really am. For what I have become today and the life I have.

For, I wasn't always like this.

Once, not very long ago, I suffered from anxiety, claustrophobia, and migraine.

My relations were in complete jeopardy. I was failing in my career.

I was unhappy, vulnerable, frustrated, and miserable.

I vividly remember that night when I was alone at home, facing my miserable thoughts, all by myself. One thought after the other, they refused to stop. The pace at which one thought flowed into another was creating havoc with my breath. It shot up and became heavier. I knew this had to stop. I was trying my best.

Finally, I gathered myself. I went into the kitchen, gulped down a glass of water and took a deep breath.

This was not the first time. Neither was it the last. The anxiety attacks had gotten the better of me since quite some time. But, now, I was determined to overcome it.

Flashback. Rewind my life to 2005

Location: Delhi Airport.

Time: An hour before the departure of my flight.

I was a bundle of nerves. Flying horrified me. But, more than that, the realization that my anxiety pill– Altrek- was missing in my bag. I was supposed to take it 45 minutes before the departure to cool down my anxious head.

I knew that there was no way that I could take off without it.

So, the next moment, I was inside a pharmacy that was located at one corner of the airport.

"Altrek please", I requested.

"Prescription please?" the chemist responded.

After all, Altrek is a serious prescription drug that can't be given over the counter.

"I don't have one", I replied, my eyes were begging for an exception.

He shook his head and denied.

My plea for mercy soon turned into desperation. My condition worsened with every moment. But, to no avail.

So, in the same condition and without popping in my saviour drug, I boarded the flight.

The moment I entered the aeroplane, I knew that I was doomed. I was palpitating, sweating, and literally crying.

I ran up to the air hostess. "I have anxiety issues. Just can't make it through the flight without Altrek" I said vehemently. "Either you get me the pill or deboard me".

The air hostess simply handed me a red towel and a glass of water.

"Wipe your face, drink water & calm down", she said. "What! This couldn't be happening to me", I thought. And then, one thought led to another.

"I have become so dependent on medicines. I can't live like this my entire life. It is getting crazier day by day. What am I leading myself into?", I thought.

I thought about my mom, who was a cardiac patient but died due to kidney problems. I was very young then. The trauma filled me with a never-ending void and drowned me into an ocean of negativity.

"I can't let history repeat itself", I thought. "My children need me and I will have to get better for them."

At that very moment, the decision was made. "This is it. I have to live a healthy life for my children", my mind repeated.

This realization hit me like a spark and there has been no looking back since then. I began to reach out for everything that could help and heal me.

I studied psychology, NLP, Reiki, Angel Healing, and Pranic Healing.

I started following Quantum Physics and Neuroplasticity to re- program my mind.

I learnt about mind, body and soul and how do they function. No learning opportunity was missed.

I got into a desperate quest for answers to a lot of questions. Some of them included: "How can I be healed? Am I born to live like this? Do I really deserve this darkness?"

There were times when I was stuck; when I did not have answers to my questions; when I could not find solutions to my life's problems. This continually inspired me to do a new course & apply its learnings on myself.

Eventually, it started working. My learnings started to create an impact on my life. My relationship with myself started improving and eventually, magic happened. My relationship with others healed. They soared. My bond with my family became stronger than ever.

My anxieties disappeared. Claustrophobia vanished. Boarding a flight became as normal as taking a breath. I was more confident.

I became happier. I thrived.

I knew it was working. My learning was actually working.

So, I started applying it to my close aids and friends. And, the results were breath-taking.

It was then that I thought that I must spread this gift to others.

So, I became a professional life coach. It was a moment of self- enlightenment. It gave me a higher purpose.

Then onwards, I was on a mission to help people identify their barriers, inspire them to reclaim their power, and love themselves by accepting their true selves.

Today, I work with thousands of people and help them in living their dreams. I help them in reviving their relationships & building up their businesses. I have been able to heal people with serious conditions like Depression, Anxiety, Piles, Asthma, Bronchitis, Gluten Allergy, and so many more. I have been able to empower them-mentally, emotionally, physically and spiritually.

Knowledge, as they say, must not be contained but passed. My life coaching school has been designed to meet this very purpose, through which I share everything that I have learnt with others who are willing to heal themselves and become certified life coaches to heal others around the world. This is how I found my way of making a difference to the world & spread smiles.

1

Fear The Genesis

'Where life is, problems are inevitable.'

Isn't that how we know life? Filled with problems–at work, home, health and relationships? We live in a constant fear of failure. The fear of not being loved, of being uncompetitive, inadequate, worthless. These problems and the fears caused by them never seem to leave us.

Workplace Problems

Today, almost 80% of the total workforce struggles with different levels of demotivation at work. 7 of every 10 employees feel disengaged at their workplace, a place where they spend almost one third of their life.

We often fall prey to the monotony of our jobs, cut-throat competition, advancement concerns, bullying, target pressures, staff attitude, ageism, negative attitudes, and so on. Then, there are other challenges that keep us on the edge—lack of quality time with family, no recognition despite hard work, monetary biases, dealing with the constant changes at work, communication barriers, differences in perspectives, and many more. For so many of us, it feels so impossible to manage our roles, responsibilities & expectations at the workplace without a conflict.

What will happen if we spend such long hours feeling demotivated and disengaged? Imagine the level of stress and anxiety being built within us! What will this frustration lead us into?

How will it impact both our personal and professional space?

THE FAILING WORK-LIFE BALANCE

About three years ago, a frustrated person approached me to find a solution. He was caught up in workplace politics and was trapped amidst gossip and red tape. His boss regularly stole the credit for his hard work and achievements and was biased towards him. The discrimination had affected his professional growth and has begun to impact his personal life as well.

Though he knew that his organization had the scope to offer him the desired growth, making it there seemed impossible due to favouritism and politics. In his zeal to make it there, he started working harder. He worked late nights for months at a stretch in the hope of a promotion.

However, the promotion never happened. Eventually, his self-confidence diminished. Frustration and regret replaced his passion and enthusiasm. He started bringing his work stress home. Slowly, this affected his relationships with his wife and children. Despite trying hard, he failed in giving them the needed attention. The whole turn of events slowly started to impact.

Finally, when he could not take anymore, he sought help.

Relationship Problems

Relationship problems are no exception in our lives. And, when we talk about relationships, it includes all—relationships with your spouse, siblings, parents, child, boss, colleagues, neighbours and everyone else that you can list down here.

The divorce rates have gone up tremendously in the last few years and an increasing number of children are forced to go through the trauma of not being protected and nurtured by both parents. Today, we can see 'parenting' emerging as a whole new subject and parents seeking guidance to raise their own children. Though, this concept was completely unheard of about 25 years ago when the parent-child relationship was nurtured naturally and stayed strong for a lifetime.

Family issues and adjustment problems with in-laws and extended families have become a common affair. There is a complete lack of empathy and trust amongst each other. Love is lost. Relations have got heavier and lost their beauty. We are feeling inadequate within ourselves. The fear of being left out all alone is taking a grip. And, all of this is eating us up from within, screaming at us and laughing aloud at how lonely and unhappy we are amidst so many people.

Health Problems

Though we don't see it like that and hardly acknowledge it, the problems at work and our relationships are slowly but certainly transmuting into health problems. It is all connected—the mind, heart and body.

The worst part is that we have labelled complex health problems such as stress, anxiety, hypertension, diabetes, thyroid and many others as lifestyle diseases and call them the 'new normal'. We have graciously accepted them as an inseparable part of our lives, letting them transform into critical illnesses such as depression, cancer, heart-attack, etc.

But is it truly normal? It is normal to be unhealthy? To lead ourselves into diseases when we can actually do something about it? Why are we not changing our lifestyle? What are we doing to protect ourselves?

Of course, the problems do not end here. In fact, they may seem endless. Though all that I have tried to do is to capture some of the most common ones and help you see which ones are you struggling with. So, let us talk about the most common problems that most of us face in our lives.

The most common problems

(a) Stress, Depression & Anxieties

We have started considering sadness and grief as normal emotions. Yes, they might be acceptable to a certain extent. But, excess of anything is bad. Isn't it?

Excessive sadness and grief take the form of stress, depression, and anxieties, which we only get to know about at the last stage, mostly when the situation has slipped our hands. The whole ordeal starts with a mood disorder or a gripping feeling of sadness and, in many cases, eventually shape up into depression—a disease which is unfortunately most common between the 18-25 age group. WHO estimates that one in every four people in the world is affected by mental or neurological disorders at some point in his/her life.

(b) Failed Relationships

With a constant increase in the cases of depression, stress, and anxiety, the number of failed relationships is also increasing. Lack of personal time, work-life imbalance and frustration at workplace are significantly contributing to this. We are failing to fulfil each-other's expectations and are unable to create happiness and love.

The result - Failed Relationships.

(c) Lifestyle Diseases

The world today is suffering largely from lifestyle diseases.

Asthma, diabetes, heart attack, piles, thyroid and similar ailments are on the rise. All of us know someone who is suffering from these. But why is it so?

Psychology says that every disease starts with an emotional imbalance and mental disorder. Lack of contentment is known to be the cause of Asthma while lack of happiness, and sweetness in life is the cause of Diabetes. Lack of love in life causes a Heart Attack. Lack of any emotion in our life builds Stress and Anxieties, each of them eventually manifesting themselves into major diseases.

(d) Fear of genetic ailments

"Take care of your heart.
Your father suffered a major stroke."
"Eat healthy, Diabetes runs in your family."

We have been hearing how our genetic structure might also be the storehouse of many hereditary diseases, and why we must do or not do something to avoid these ailments. The fear of genetic disorders is a deep-rooted fear planted early-on in our subconscious mind, and troubles us every now and then. And, when we keep repeating it to ourselves, the fear grips us further, and we end up manifesting the disorders within us.

(e) Directionless Life

Lack of direction is the biggest problem and reason for fear in life, especially, when a person has a goal, but no direction. To have the right direction in life, it is important to have the right mentor. To have the right mentor, you should have the courage to accept your fear and the need for a mentor. To have that courage and acceptance, this book will become your mentor.

(f) Cut-throat Competition

"Life is a race. Run, or you will lose."

How many times have you heard these words? At every stage of your life–be it your first independent step, competitive examination, first paycheque, career, and more. The cut-throat competition is our biggest hurdle. The preparation for winning takes over everything, and we forget to live in the moment. Not to mention the 'loser tag' that you get labelled with and all the emotional and mental pain that you suffer in case you lose the race.

(g) No family life

Unfortunately, we have equated success to financial stability, not happiness. This form of success allows little time to talk and stay connected with those that matter the most. Our fast-paced lives leave no opportunity to spend quality time with our family. In a scenario, when we are unable to spare enough time for our spouse and children, managing time for parents and grandparents becomes out of equation. Soon, the happiness of financial success starts fading away, and we are surrounded by grief and loneliness.

Do any of these problems sound familiar? Have you been dealing with them?

Many of us have dealt with more than one of these or are still struggling with them. The surprising part is that, over a period of time, we have accepted them as a part of our routine life. They seem to be like a natural by-product of our work lives or failing relationships.

This, my friend, is the real problem.

Actual trouble starts when we don't realize that the problem has crossed the threshold of any one aspect of our life, and started interfering with many other aspects.

Today, 40% of the workforce report high-stress levels at work. Though it is an alarming number, they have considered it as a part of their life. However, the mind and body are reacting otherwise.

Let us try to understand what happens when we get caught up in an undesirable work schedule or a bad relationship.

- We lose track of our actions
- We don't know what to do & how to react
- We lose our self-esteem, our confidence, and the sight of our life's aim
- The clarity of life vanishes
- We get confused
- We make wrong choices at work and life
- We eventually mess up with our priorities and everything else

Though, all of this happens at a subconscious level, a scenario where we are not making any conscious choices or acting in awareness, our body feels the brunt. The emotional turmoil within us, knowingly or unknowingly, begins to affect our mental health & physical well-being. Resultantly, Hypertension,

Insomnia, Blood Pressure issues, Headaches, Stomach Problems and Body Pains take birth in our body.

Is there any limit to this? Does the impact of a bad work-life or stressed relationship end here?

No! I have also seen it culminating into critical diseases and go as far as a cardiac arrest.

Not just this. The impact goes beyond physical ailments and can also cause mental problems. Mental disorders such as Anxiety and Depression are the next in queue. Emotional Disregulation, Hormonal Imbalance, Irritability, and similar things also tend to make a permanent place in our life as we struggle to fight the external challenges in our life.

Slowly, as we are gripped by our Stress, Anxieties, mental and physical ailments, the direct impact is felt on our relationships. They start turning sour. We start blaming and fighting with our families for unbelievable and irrational reasons. Frustration leads to fights. We feel that they don't understand us. We stop spending time with them. We ignore them and try to find solace elsewhere. Slowly, the lack of love and companionship starts eating us up alive and ruins our mental balance & physical health further. Eventually, we get into a vicious loop where our problems at one place start affecting our entire life.

Where do problems originate from?

Now we know that all of us are suffering from one problem or the other. But where do these problems originate from? What is the reason behind so much Stress and Anxiety?

Let us list down a few of them:

- We want instant gratification and have no patience
- We feel that we are not good enough and that the others are better

- We expect a lot from others
- We want our relationships to work automatically
- We want easy promotions
- We have become less humane and lost our emotional connect with other humans
- We have lost our core existential values, and made our lives more dependent on the materialistic world than trying to raise our own consciousness
- The insane show-off and comparison on social media, and the constant pressure of living a life that others are projecting on their social media accounts
- The habit of blaming others for our problems
- Guilt of being a reason behind someone else's problems

Whatever be the reason, the problem arising from it is not as big as it seems. However, your mind is creating a story in your head and making the problem look larger than life. In reality, the situation may be only 10% on the outside and 90% in your head.

Nobody was born with a guarantee card of a smooth life—without troubled relationships, breakdowns, or financial turbulence. This is a normal part of life but we are not ready to accept it. Why are we giving so much significance to things around us? Why are we attaching unnecessary meaning to our thoughts? And by doing all these, why are we creating unnecessary stress in our life?

How to handle stress?

What can you do to get over the 'larger than life' problem that you have created? How can you minimize the stress caused by it and turn around your situation?

The situation will never change but your thoughts can

It's important for us to understand that the situation will never change. All that you can ever do is to train your brain to think positive. Ask it to focus on the good things and solutions instead of the problems. Train it to give up negative thoughts and start living in the present moment.

Press the pause button. Analyse the situation. See what can be done.

What do you do when your child behaves badly or talks in an objectionable language? Don't you immediately stop your child?

Likewise, our brain is our child. We have to stop our brain to think excessively about the problems by showing it how much we love it. Request your brain and say: "You should pay attention to something positive my dear." Repeat it again and again. You need to train your mind to pause and shift its focus to something positive at that moment, the present moment.

Be the master of your own mind. Do things that make you happy. Listen to happy music. Spend time with loved ones. Eat and drink healthy food. Love yourself.

We always have a choice

What we want to think and how much, is completely our choice. We have a complete choice on whether to react or keep mum. We have the power to control and give direction to our thought process and choose our thoughts accordingly. Then, why not choose the best!

Think like this—if you have the power to choose everything, what will you choose for yourself—Stress or Joy? The answer is obvious.

We all live in a friendly and abundant Universe. A Universe that really wants to contribute towards whatever we desire. All that we need is to keep enough patience and positivity to reach out for our goals.

Never give up on your dreams. Stay away from negative influence. Use your energy wisely. Channelize it to create something powerful. Be in gratitude for basic things in life, and live a happy and cheerful life.

The power belongs to you. Make the right choice. Only you yourself can change your life.

How do we usually overcome our problems?

We now know that the best way to deal with a problem is to first deal with your mind. But are we actually doing that? Have you ever questioned your thoughts when stuck amidst a bad situation?

No. Then what do you do? Chances are that we do one of the following in search for a solution:

- Go to the doctor
- Visit a therapist
- Blame and complain
- Consult astrologers/tarot card readers
- Change jobs
- Break our marriage
- Find another client
- Give up

With all the frustration clouding our logical thinking, a lot of us blame the problems and call them our bad luck. The easiest way out is to run away from the situation and ignore it. Or approach an astrologer, numerologist, tarot card reader, etc.

Few of us might choose to go to our closest friend & confide in them, seeking their advice on what they think about our situation in their own mind. But do you really think that they can give us any viable solution without putting their foot into our shoes? What is the probability of them giving you the right solution? God forbid, if you actually apply it to your personal or professional life, you can get into a deeper mess.

Some of us might also consider looking for a solution on the internet or attending various workshops where the trainer has no clue about what you are going through. The most that you can expect is a standard 'one size fits all' advice. With generalized information all over the internet and no customized solution to your problem, chances are that you will be left more confused, directionless & frustrated than before.

Then, there are situations when we become workaholic and begin to ignore every other aspect of life. We keep working day and night, spoiling our work-life balance further and making our life a complete mess. We switch our job, believing that the new office will be a perfect place with perfect people, rendering us free of office politics, favouritism, and many other workplace evils. And soon, we are jolted out of our dreams to face reality again. Once that happens, we tell ourselves- "it's alright, I can manage my day at work if I can compensate for the craziness elsewhere." So, we start going out on every weekend, socializing, indulging in clubbing, late night parties, etc, and eventually fall into a deeper mess.

Whatever we do, no matter which path we choose, nothing works. Nothing brings peace of mind. In fact, most of them give temporary relief, before we bounce back to a higher level of frustration. The whole thing breaks us & makes us feel worthless.

Frustrated and tired of all the trials, we finally begin to ignore everything that comes our way and find it easier to let go of things. We develop a "it is all hopeless and dark out there, so why try" attitude.

The boss is shouting- let go; promotion is due but not happening- let go; the wife is complaining- let go; the child is crying- let go. A habit of letting go develops unknowingly. In the event, we learn to let go of everything which meant the whole world to us once upon a time, and we become more aloof than ever.

What is the outcome of all of these? What finally happens? The list of losses is endless, and all of this for a zero improvement in our situation.

- Loss of money
- Loss of time
- Loss of energy
- Loss of peace of mind
- Loss of joy
- Loss of emotional health
- Loss of mental health
- Loss of physical health

What can we do to overcome our problems?

The biggest irony is that we feel someone outside of us is responsible for our misery. We complain and blame others. We blame our circumstances, our upbringing, opportunities, people, etc. We go in denial, unwilling to accept that as much the problem is ours, so is the opportunity to overcome it and live a better life.

We want our lives to get better but we don't want to change our habits and our inner world. "Wouldn't it be better if the people and situation around us could change?", we think.

How can that be? How can changing something else change your life?

Can anything truly stopping us from realizing our dreams if we have the will power and potential to achieve it?

Truth be told—our outer reality will only change if we change our inner realty.

Now is time to be willing to change.

If we really want something around us to change, we must change inside. We must change our way of thinking, speaking, and expressing ourselves. These inner changes will then change what we manifest in our outer world.

Life is all about upgrading ourselves. We all have lessons to learn.

The next question is how do we initiate this change? Awareness is the first step in healing or changing ourselves. Think like this—if we want to move from one room to another, we have to first be aware of our desire and then accomplish it by getting up from our chair, and then standing up to go to another room. Unless you know what you desire, what is stopping you to achieve it and what are the steps that you can take to fulfil it, will you ever be able to make it to the other room?

Since childhood, we have been conditioned to see things and live in a certain way. If our parents fought, we grew up thinking that it is normal to fight and have trouble in relationships. If we saw people around us being dominated by their boss and giving up easily, we believed that this is how work life is supposed to be. If we saw our friends and relatives popping up pills every now and then, we started taking our health for granted and began to accept stress and anxiety as a normal part of the routine. But is accepting any of this as a part of our routine normal? Or, should we raise an alarm and make a conscious choice to change it?

The most important thing, therefore, is to identify our problems as problems, and not normal. Once we are able to do this, we will be able to accept them and do something about them. We will learn that there are other ways to live, to handle a relationship, or build a healthy body than what we have always known and believed. We will know that something has to change for our life to change.

Once we learn how to get to this level of awareness, we will have a choice to change things and see life in a different light. We will have the choice to either remain disempowered, dissatisfied, unhappy and live an unfulfilled life or to change things within us, create opportunities, be happy and live a life of our dreams.

Believe me when I say that you can do this, all by yourself. Yes, you do not have to go anywhere or change anyone or anything around you. That would be insane. How many people or circumstances will you change? And, why would you? Why would anyone else or the world change to bring you the happiness that you seek?

It is your life, your life story and your script. If anything has to change in this, it is you, yourself. You will have to be the change you wish to manifest in your life. As we just said, 'changing your inner reality will change your outer reality'.

All of us have the ability to change our environment and our perception regarding the environment. Our mind is the lens of our perception. By changing our mind, overcoming fear, and the beliefs or constraints that we hold within ourselves, we have the ability to change our health, and how we experience life.

In fact, when you take a closer look at your problems, you will know that all of them emerge from the negative thoughts hiding secretly inside your inner reality.

YOUR INNER REALITY CREATES YOUR OUTER REALITY

Once there lived a king very far away. One day when he was taking a tour of his kingdom, a thorn pricked one of his feet and it started bleeding. Anxious, the king wanted to fix to this problem. So, he asked his artisans to cover the entire kingdom with a velvet cloth. Alas! That was an impossible task and everyone failed miserably at it.

The king didn't know what to do and called upon many wise men to advice him on the problem. At last, one wise old man then came up with a noble solution. He said " when it is you who has a problem, why are you trying to cover the entire kingdom with velvet. It is your feet that needs to be fixed and not the places that you visit. How about covering your feet with velvet?"

The king loved the idea and acted upon it immediately. He thanked the old man profusely and never ever did his feet bleed again.

What worked for the king in this story?

He took charge of his own problem and fixed it within himself instead of trying to change his outer circumstances.

Your thought and its outcome

(a) Thought: I am not good enough

Outcome:

- No recognition at workplace
- Average marks in school
- Trouble in relationships

(b) Thought: Money does not grow on trees

Outcome:

- Lack of financial success
- Less career opportunities

(c) Thought: Good things don't last forever

Outcome:

- Short-lived happiness
- Unstable relationships

At the bottom of all these thoughts lies a single most emotion–the emotion of fear.

In fact, there are only two basic underlying emotions behind everything that we think, feel and do-the emotions of Fear and Love.

FEAR means 'False Evidence Appearing Real'. It's the only thing that creates a barrier between you and your growth. It is the underlying for every negative emotion and experience in your life.

On the other end, everything positive that you experience emerges from the emotion of Love. Love expands your energy. It helps you to rise and be in an acceptance mode.

Now that we know that being in Love is a wiser choice, the questions are:

- How to be in an expansion state forever?
- How to beat fear and stay in the positive light of love?

As the popular saying goes- 'it is very important to know about your enemy before you can defeat it ('fear' in this case).' So, how can you fight with fear without learning about it and then acquiring the apt skills to conquer it?

We can only win against fear if we know:

- How does fear look like?
- How many different varieties and variations does it have?
- What are its strategies?
- What loss can it cause to your life?
- And everything else that you can possibly find out

So, let us approach the first step of conquering fear-understanding it. I am sure that by the end of this book, you will know fear not as your enemy, but as your friend.

Relationship between stress, fear & anxiety

Fear is the perception of danger. Danger, here, means any perceived threat that has the potential to cause you psychological, physiological, emotional, or spiritual harm.

Fear (the perception of danger) is often experienced across different levels by different individuals. For example:

- **Little to mild fear** can be experienced as nervousness, concern, or apprehension;
- **Mild to moderate fear** can be experienced as agitation, anxiety, and worry, and;

- **Moderate to extreme fear** is often experienced as being frightened, scared, terrified, or hysterical.

Fear is very closely connected to stress.

Unfortunately, not many people see the connection. That is because they only identify fear as fear when it reaches the third level–moderate to extreme—and experience it in the form of being frightened, terrified, scared, or afraid. They overlook the fact that fear has variations and can also be expressed through low to moderate emotions of worry, concern, agitation, and anxiety.

Nonetheless, fear at any level, produces acute stress responses and therefore creates undue stress on the body. The degree of stress is directly proportional to the degree of fear. Abnormal levels of fear and anxiety can cause significant distress and dysfunction and limit a person's ability to experience the joy of life.

So, next time, whenever you are nervous, concerned, worried, or fretful, know that it is not just like any other passing emotion, and is causing immense stress to your body.

Nearly one in every four people experience a form of anxiety disorder during their lives, and nearly 8 percent experience post-traumatic stress disorder (PTSD). Disorders of anxiety and fear include Phobias, Social Phobia, Generalized Anxiety Disorder, Separation Anxiety, PTSD, and Obsessive-Compulsive Disorder.

These conditions usually begin at a young age, and without appropriate treatment, can become chronic and debilitating, and affect a person's life trajectory. The good news is that we have effective treatments that work in a relatively short time period, in the form of psychotherapy and medications.

Fear manifests into diseases

Many of us can now understand that physical symptoms and illnesses often begin first in the emotional and mental bodies. We are not just a physical body. We also have an aura of subtle bodies including the etheric, mental, emotional, astral, and causal. Energy healers, clairvoyants, and shamans are able to feel or see these bodies.

It is important to understand that our emotions and thoughts are energy. If the E-MOTIONS are not expressed 'in motion' they can get stuck within our body causing a block in energy flow. Any trauma or inherited cellular memory can also result in less than optimal functioning of the meridians of Chi or Prana flowing through the body.

Both Hypochondriasis' and 'Nomophobia' are fears of illness. The difference is in the exact nature of the fear. Nosophobia is the fear of developing a selected disease like cancer or diabetes, whereas Hypochondriasis is the fear that existing physical symptoms could also be the result of an undiagnosed disease.

Though our western system of 'Allopathic Medicine' can offer emergency life-saving surgeries, as well as subdue and control symptoms, the root cause of our disease is often not addressed. On the other hand, Reiki and other modalities that work around the energy field, can have lasting healing results by gently unblocking the stuck energies which are causing the illness. Shamanic Techniques, which have been the traditional form of physical and psychic healing for thousands of years, can also remove dark energy intrusions, spirit attachments, and offer soul retrieval through energy healing and plant medicine. These modalities, coupled with counselling and lifestyle changes, show that holistic treatments offer a more sustainable and lasting form of healing. There are many current studies to prove that energy healing works.

2

An Audience With Fear

If you search the word "Fear", Google will pop up a multitude of definitions. Of those, the one that explains it as an acronym (FEAR), helps us to understand the word as is. As per the acronym, the definition of the word is:

F-False

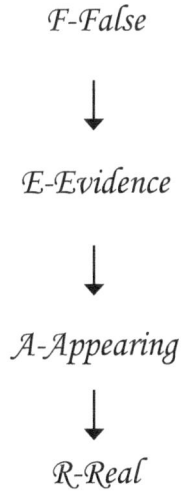

E-Evidence

A-Appearing

R-Real

Fear is an emotional baggage, which is imperative to carry, given that it comes into frequent use. It varies in nature, extent, and time duration. Sometimes it is mild, sometimes severe, sometimes small and at other times big. It can be ephemeral or long-lasting and comes in various forms and levels.

> *"The only thing we have to fear is fear itself- nameless, unreasoning, unjustified, terror which paralyzes needed efforts to convert retreat in advance".*
>
> *–Franklin D. Roosevelt*

Is fear inherited from the environment or is it ancestral?

Though this topic may open a long debate having people arguing for both—acquired as well as genetic—but I have good reasons to believe that fear is ingrained in the nervous system, and it is instinctive.

It all starts with the survival instincts we all are endowed with. You might have seen so many examples in the world around you, one of it is an infant crying the moment he/she senses something unpleasant in his/her environment. As age progresses, this survival instinct of an infant gets fortified and is couple with many other things that we experience in life.

Fear is one of the most basic human emotion, and I think that its very purpose in us, and all other living communities, is to promote survival and to protect us from danger. It is like a gene that passes from one generation to the next, a reason why every child is born with fear.

Human beings are born with two fears Two fears are inherited in babies and passed to them through the womb of their mother. We grow up with them unknowingly and unconsciously.

- The fear of falling down, and;
- The fear of loud noises.

An experiment was done in the 1960s where in new-borns were placed on a platform which had a diaphanous plexiglass extension. As soon as the babies reached the edge of the platform, they stopped due to the fear of falling off. This proved that all babies have a certain level of hereditary consciousness and are scared of falling down.

Similarly, if babies are suddenly hurled in the air by a stranger, the act invokes a startling response in them. On the contrary, when they are hurled in the air by their parents and are expecting it, they learn to enjoy it. This happens since they receive positive vibrations from their parents, which assures them of being in safe hands.

Talking about the second inborn fear—the fear of loud noise—it's interesting to note that new-born babies get startled, when they hear loud noises. This is because a loud noise sends the message of a possible danger to our brain. It invokes a response known as an 'acoustic startle reflex' which usually makes us put our heads down, and directs our body to shrink to avoid any possible jeopardy.

Though science tells us that human beings are fearful of loud noises, spirituality tells us why humans are born with this fear. As per spirituality, the original nature of our spirit is 'peacefulness'. Thus, loud voices make us uneasy, and we try to block it by placing our hands firmly on our ears.

All other fears—apart from that of falling down and of loud noises—are gathered by us from our environment during childhood and adulthood. We inherit these fears from our families, our friends, our culture, our environment, and our life's experiences. As we grow up, these acquired fears become a part of our personality, and keep changing in their form and levels.

There is a very common saying that "we are the average of five people we are in association with". This saying is apt here as our fears and thereby our personality and our lives are a sum total of the people, we spend most time with. Here are a few ways and situations through which fear gets ingrained in our minds:

- Superstitions discussed within the family give birth to a superstitious mind, and we develop related fears since our childhood.

- In childhood, if we do not study well, our parents start feeding our minds with the fear of failure which scares us till much later in life.

- As we grow up, we develop the fear of losing our jobs. We fear being fired for being straightforward. So, we speak less, listen more and agree to everything that our boss says, irrespective of being right or wrong.

- Fear of meeting an accident stops us from learning to drive or sometimes walk on the road.

Once, a girl visited me to be healed. She was 30 years' old and single. She suffered from the fear of walking on the road as she believed that the moment she would do that, someone would hit her. She also suffered from nightmares in which she saw herself being hit by a car or a truck on the road.

I took her back to her childhood through my healing techniques.

I asked her to recall the first time when she experienced this fear.

She went back in time when she was about six years old, and was returning from school, holding her father's hand. She wanted to walk free but her father was reluctant of letting her do so. So, he held on to her firmly.

After some time, she told her father that she wanted to eat an ice-cream. While they were crossing the road to buy an ice-cream, her father's grip loosened accidentally and the girl took it as an opportunity to move freely on the road. She achieved her goal and started roaming in the middle of the road while her father got information about danger, and when you know the nature as well as the intensity of the threat.

If the opinions expressed by the psychologists of today are to be believed, our fear response is an ancient instinct, unaffected by the nuances of modern civilization. Though the nature of fear has changed, the quantum of fear and our response to it has remained the same through ages.

During early civilizations, humans had to fight ferocious animals to survive in the forest. Though there were caves for shelter, they did not translate into complete protection. The element of fear, thus troubled its inmates throughout the night.

As we progressed, the nature of threat changed. Today, we tend to fear unhygienic water, food, pollution, uncultured people, loss of job, earthquake, theft of valuables, money, losing a person, etc. We are arguably more vulnerable today than we were hundreds of years ago. The nature of fear has changed but not the fear itself. Undoubtedly, even today, our fear protects us as it protected us centuries ago.

However, that does not mean that you should run away from all fearful situations. Sometimes, fear is important to just get a person into action. Fear of failure brings sincerity in a student and helps him to study harder; the fear of losing job brings discipline and a sense of responsibility in an adult, and likewise.

> *"Not too much, not too less, have me as per your need. I will save you from performing sins, and will always balance your karmic account".*
>
> *—Fear*

3

Fears Come From Beliefs

Are you afraid of failure? Or perhaps you have a fear of success? Do you feel that you cannot truly realize your lifelong dreams?

"Of course yes! Who isn't scared? Being in fear is natural", you might say.

But why is it so natural? How do we build these fears? Where does it all begin?

To understand this better, let us travel back in time and go back to our childhood.

Remember, how as a child, we had this great sense of adventure? A wild imagination and the 'devil may care' attitude!

When exactly did this enthusiasm dampen? When did we quit dreaming big and stopped taking risks?

As we grow up—more often than not- we are programmed to stop dreaming and think more responsibly and more realistically. Perhaps we were told that "no-one from our town makes it big" or maybe someone said that "girls are meant to stay at home and raise a family". We heard these 'so-called opinions' so often and saw so many living examples that resonated with what we heard, that these thoughts and opinions got embedded deep into our subconscious. This later became our belief system and gave birth to our very own limited beliefs.

Limiting Beliefs are the ideas that we believe to be true, even though in fact, they might just be an opinion; opinions that we have formed from years and years of negative talk, both from ourselves and relatives full of good intentions. Here are some examples of limiting beliefs:

- "I can't lose weight"
- "I will never find the right partner"
- "I am not good enough for a promotion"

Almost every fear comes from our belief system, such as—fear of rejection, fear of not being good enough, fear of failure, and fear of superstitions. Our beliefs are imbibed in our subconscious mind since we are born and sometimes much before while we are still developing in our mother's womb.

While our conscious mind makes us aware of our surroundings and processes the present information, our subconscious mind is operating silently behind the scenes. From childhood experiences to past memories, tons of information is being processed below the realm of conscious awareness. Since we are not mindful of these happenings, our emotions can be quite irrational. Our fears also reside in the subconscious mind. It is only by getting some handle on our subconscious mind that we can hope to get rid of it.

The big difference between feeling fearful and letting our fears hold us back

By acknowledging our fears, we can fight our limiting beliefs. It is the first step towards making the necessary changes that can help us to achieve desired results. By changing our beliefs, we can, therefore, change our reality.

For example, altering our thoughts from—"I can't lose weight" to "my own health and fitness are in my control"—may allow us the freedom to take control again. Just one shift in our thought can give us an option to change our habits and behaviours, and open up the possibility to live a healthier life. The solution can be as simple as eliminating sugar in your tea or walking 15 minutes a day.

Again, changing the limiting belief of "I will never find the right partner" to "there are so many people out there who could be right for me", gives us the opportunity to make changes and allows us to recognize such possibilities. The solution can be to join a gym or a sports club which can open up your social circle, and widen your possibilities.

In both cases, what did we do? We just replaced our negative thought with a positive one.

In any situation, the trick is to replace our negativity with positivity.

New thoughts =New beliefs = New results

Change is not always easy, but where there is no challenge–there is no change. These changes do not have to be earth-shattering – but by opening up our mind a little–these changes have the potential to create a huge difference.

How is fear ingrained in a child's mind?

When a toddler is born, they need no logic, reason, or inhibitory processes. They use primitive mechanisms to help us understand their needs. The only fears a baby is born with are the fear of falling and the fear of loud noises. All other fears are learned over the years via identification and association.

From age zero to approximately eight, the kid develops a library of those identifications and associations. They learn that a number of these are good (positive) and a few are bad (negative). These positive and negative associations become the life script of the kid. It is formed from what they know despite the fact that the kid doesn't yet know how to differentiate the right from wrong.

Identifications cause associations that cause emotions. For example, if a toddler has had a scary experience with a dog in his past, the identification is the dog, the experience is frightening, and the emotion is fear. Therefore, the toddler's script reads that identification of a dog results in the association of danger that results in the emotion of fear.

Children are very receptive from the time they are born till they are 8 years old. Most of their beliefs are formed in early years from what they see, hear, and grab. During this time, their right brain is active and their left brain–which is responsible for logic, critical thinking, language and physical activities–is not yet fully functional. (In fact, scientists now believe that brains aren't fully developed until we are well into our twenties, possibly even our thirties.) Your child is 'programmed' for his adult years during this phase of development and it is this subconscious 'programming' that will run 95% of his adult life. It is from the age of 0-8 that children acquire limiting beliefs, which later limit their opportunities and sabotages their success.

For instance, if a child grows up in a household where parents keep repeating that "if you don't get good grades in class, you'll never have a good job", he may grow up with a subconscious belief that " I do not deserve a good job because I didn't give my best in school".

From the age of eight to approximately twelve, a toddler starts to develop logic and reason. The child is now capable of making decisions and developing will power. This becomes the conscious mind and represents around 10% of the mind. The subconscious still represents the remaining 90% of the mind.

An important aspect that parents should remember is that the subconscious has no sense of humour. It is not logical and it takes things literally. It doesn't interpret. When parents joke with their children, or maybe worse, use sarcasm, that is very real for the children. Statements like "Are you stupid?" or "Leave me alone!" are not interpreted but taken as truth.

It is important to realize that there is an immediate connection between how kids feel and the way they behave. When kids feel right, they'll behave right.

So, how can we help them to feel right?

The answer is—by accepting their feelings and helping them to correct their life script.

The problem is that parents and other elders do not usually accept their children's feelings (without even realizing it). We often shove it off by saying.

- "You don't really feel that way."
- "You're just saying that because you're tired."
- "There's no reason to be so upset."

Steady denial of feelings can confuse and enrage kids. It also teaches them not to know what their feelings are—not to trust them.

It is critical to note that if we do not take the developmental phase of the kid 's mind into serious consideration and behave in alignment to his needs, he might end up creating a life script and subconscious programming that would hinder his growth and progress.

A CHILD'S BRAIN

A child's critical mind only develops around the age of eight, therefore whatever they hear, see, and feel goes directly into the subconscious without analysis, and is accepted as fact. As the subconscious never sleeps, the quantity of knowledge that goes directly into their subconscious is phenomenal. In the eyes of your child, you're literally everything, and within the programmable Theta state (4-8 Hz.) whatever you tell them, their brain will record as true.

So, until the age of eight, the brain is merely downloading data. Are you afraid of heights? Do you believe that money doesn't grow on trees or that love hurts? Chances are that those beliefs were instilled in you unwittingly by your parents when your mind was still malleable and unable to contest. It was unable to contest because, until eight years of age, brain frequency patterns are dominated by Theta waves, holding the kid during a hypnagogic trance. This trance-like state allows everything that happens before birth through eight years to travel directly into the subconscious—bypassing the conscious mind. In other words, at this age, the brain is merely downloading data and therefore the critical mind isn't yet working.

The conscious and subconscious mind

The conscious mind sees with the eyes. It perceives the outside experiences. For instance, it is your conscious mind that sees this web page.

The subconscious, on the opposite hand, has no contact with the surface world. It is blind.

The subconscious mind relies on sensory input. Thus, it responds to reality and imagination in the same way. Younger children, who operate through their subconscious minds, are especially vulnerable as they absorb and accept both negative and positive influences with equal energy. If your child's belief structure is based largely on fears, lack of confidence, a sense of rejection or inadequacy, the decisions made by their conscious mind will in turn, reflect those beliefs.

The good news is that the parent's mistakes can be undone.

What does belief mean?

Beliefs are rules or rituals that we create to live a life.

Often, they are so deeply ingrained into our subconscious that we never think about them at a conscious level. However, these beliefs signify our behaviour, consciously or subconsciously, and, over the time, become a part of our personality.

The world is what you believe it to be. Your whole world rolls around your belief. You take all your decisions based on your beliefs, either personal or professional.

Taking a simple example: if you believe that people are inherently mean and selfish, then you doubt them and you will actively look for evidence that supports that belief. And you will find it!

Instead, if you believe that people are inherently good and are trying their best, then you may blindly trust them. And you will find ways to explain people's behaviour that support that belief.

So, you can go on and keep holding onto the beliefs that you've grown up with—that you've been taught through your upbringing and your education—or you can recognize them for what they are, i.e. beliefs. With this new perspective, you are now free to create new beliefs and change your behaviour accordingly.

Beliefs in the world of work and career

Let us look at a few other examples of beliefs, specifically in the context of the 9 to 5 corporate life.

Examples of beliefs around the way of working:

- "Having an employer gives me security"
- "It's safer to stay in a 9 to 5 job"
- "Work isn't supposed to be enjoyable"

Examples of beliefs around your goals:

- "It's irresponsible to go after what I want"
- "I have too many passions"
- "It'll never happen"

Examples of beliefs around money:

- "You can't earn a lot of money doing the work that you love"
- "Creative work pays less"
- "Rich people are selfish and greedy"

Examples of beliefs around your own abilities:

- "I'm not entrepreneurial"
- "It may work for others but not for me because of X reason"

- "I can't do it"

Examples of beliefs around your growth and development:

- "I should be able to do this by myself"
- "Asking for help is a sign of weakness"
- "I can't afford to invest in myself"

Yes, these are beliefs. However, they are not irrefutable facts, and are only true to the extent that you believe in them.

Challenging your beliefs

As you take a look at your beliefs around life, family, relationships, health, work and career and money, you need to ask yourself: "Do I want to keep believing in these?"

And, if the answer is "no"–then the next step is to change them! The point here is that you have a choice. You can choose to continue with your existing beliefs, existing behaviours and existing results. Or, you can choose to change those beliefs, create new behaviours and enjoy different results.

We know that it can be quite scary to challenge a fundamental belief that you have held for as long as you can remember. It can shake the very foundation on which your life, or even your identity, has been built. And it will mean taking ownership of your choices instead of blaming your parents, society, or any other external reason that you have been holding onto for why you are not able to do what you really want to do.

Though, take solace in knowing that whenever you choose to change a belief, the effect can be immediate. You can simply choose to believe something else – and that's it! Once you have opened your eyes to a different perspective, you will find more and more evidence to support your new belief.

Again, some examples here:

Change your beliefs

- From "having an employer gives me security" to "working for myself will give me more security as I'll be on top of the things."

- From "work isn't supposed to be enjoyable" to "work isn't supposed to be miserable."

- From "it will never happen" to "I will find how to make it happen."

Of course, it may not be that simple and you may find yourself behaving in a way that still reflects one of your old beliefs. If so, take a deep breath and remind yourself that this is no longer a belief that you hold – and choose to change your behaviour accordingly.

Worst case, you can fake it until you make it!

Think to yourself: "how would I act if I believed something different?". For instance, "what would I do if I believe that I am good enough?" or "what would I do if I believe that working for myself can offer more security than working for an employer?" Then see the new possibilities that crop up with a mere shift in belief.

Every thought you have, every belief you believe in, is a choice. Changing your beliefs will change your behaviour. This is what will allow you to achieve those big dreams that might previously have seemed completely unattainable.

4

Faced By Imaginary Fears

In Mahabharata, Yakshya asked Yudhishthira– "What is the biggest illusion that humans have?"

Yudhishthira replied-

"The biggest illusion of humans is that they know they have to die but they live as they will never die".

As we discussed in the previous chapter, only two fears are inborn and all other fears are inherited from the society and our environment.

If we divide them further into categories, fears are of two kinds: real and imaginary.

What is real fear?

When things happen in real and where there is a real danger, it is real fear. This fear is genuine. Few examples may include fears which are visible like the fear that we experience when we are stuck amidst fire, Tsunami, flood, or any other natural calamity.

All other fears than real fear are imaginary fears. 98% of our fears are imaginary.

How do we identify if the fear is real or imaginary? Observe the conversation. When the conversation has an element of "if this happens then what", it is an imaginary fear. For example; what if I die, how will my family survive? What if I lose a part of my body?"

These are imaginary fears.

Types of imaginary fears

1. The fear of inadequacy

People who suffer from the fear of inadequacy feel insufficient within themselves. They have low confidence, and a lack of ability to deal with the situation. They keep complaining about life. They keep questioning life. For example,

- "Why did it happen to me?"
- "Why does this always happen to me?"
- "I can't talk in front of them, it is scary."

2. The fear of uncertainty

This fear is about demolition, of desisting to exist. This is equivalent to the fear of death. The fear that 'we would no longer be alive someday' strikes at the very heart of our being. People who experience this fear may frequently be worried about:

- "How will I die?"
- "Will I live long or not?"
- "Will I be able to accomplish all my goals before I die?"

They are scared of looking over the edge of a tall building, flying, heights and mortal diseases. They may even resist going to the doctor. They are people who fear rats, lizards, spiders, dogs, snakes or any other animal that they believe is harmful. These are symptoms of anxieties caused due to uncertainty.

Remember the story I shared about the girl who met an accident in her childhood but was carrying her anxiety in her adulthood? It points out to this fear of uncertainty.

3. The fear of failure

The most popular fear in adulthood is the fear of failure. Here a person feels worthless, ashamed, or humiliated. This fear, as we talked about earlier, is usually an outcome of undue pressure from our adults while we are still children-

- Pressure to come first in class
- Comparison with other kids
- Being blamed for scoring just 1% less in exams
- Pressure to behave well

Many suicide cases are registered every year due to the fear of failure.

4. The fear of rejection

This type of fear is called "EGO-DEATH" as it makes a person feel victimized, criticized and heart-broken.

Examples of this include a student who feels rejected after being teased in school or bullied in college. This fear is also very common amongst people, whose love and proposal are rejected, in turn leaving them with a feeling of lifelong rejection. The fear of rejection is also inbuilt within certain people due to their culture, which nurture different beliefs about casteism, racism, religion, etc.

Truth be told, we have misunderstood the difference between ego and self-respect, thus creating the fear of rejection. If we understand the true meaning of self- respect, we will never feel rejected.

I am feeling rejected
I am feeling rejected because I am dark
I am feeling rejected because I am not from
the majority I am feeling rejected because I was raped
I am feeling rejected because I was criticized
I am feeling rejected because I was bullied for fun
I am feeling rejected because
I was rejected
I am feeling rejected.

5. The fear of missing out

Unfortunately, social media has become an active platform to win fame and recognition, a place which gives us a sense of completion. It has become compulsive to share our life, and its events on social media, else we suffer the fear of missing out. We are on our mobile phone first thing in the morning. So much so, that it has distracted us from our real goals. The magnitude of the fear of missing out is forcing people to invest their productive and valuable time on social media.

But, is it truly worth it?

Are we not actually missing out on our real self in this madness of being ever-present on the virtual world? Think about it.

6. The fear of change

The fear of change is the top reason to resist change. This fear occurs due to a change in place, people, technology, etc. and is usually an outcome of the old belief system which perceives change as a threat and directs us to resist it.

This fear is most seen in the elderly segment who, over a period of time, get habitual to a particular place, particular people, particular things, and a particular belief system. You may have noticed old parents shifting from their native villages to a city. How do they feel? Uncomfortable, isn't it? They resist going to the city because they have spent their entire life in the village in a certain way, which

will no longer be possible if they switch to a city. Change is hard for them.

The fear of change is also common amongst adults when they join a new office which warrants them to learn updated technology and new protocols. You might often notice them trying to break the new protocols and resist this change.

7. The fear of losing control

The fear of losing control brings the fear of losing the authority, fear of losing people, fear of losing position in a job and, fear of losing control over people in the family.

Fear of losing authority and control is very common amongst older family members and old females. The female members of the family behave rudely with their daughter- in-law because they fear losing authority within their home. Similarly, mothers experience the fear of losing their son, hence they build conspiracies after their marriage. Again, people on top-positions have the fear of losing their edge and thus indulge in office politics. Similarly, people in middle roles experience the fear of losing their job, so they flatter their boss.

8. The fear of being judged

Fear of being judged is very common across all age groups except in children. Children are unaware of this fear. It takes birth on account of poverty, own belief systems, inferiority complex, etc. The fear of being judged proves that we lack self-love.

Hiding your feelings, protecting your image, not speaking your heart out are a few common symptoms of living in the fear of being judged.

9. The fear that something bad will happen

Our imagination is so powerful that it can create anything after experiencing a visual. For example, if you have watched a scary movie and are continuously thinking about it, it can become a nightmare for you. A nightmare can later be converted into the fear that something bad will happen to you.

A person suffering from hallucinations once came to me for healing. In his imagination, he used to see his house on fire and his family caught up and dying in it. It troubled him to an extent that he believed it to be true.

We feel bodily invasion or mutilation while being caught up in this fear. It might include the fear of losing a part of our body, fear of organ dysfunction or the fear of breaking bones within our body. In this fear, we feel physically unsafe or under an attack.

5

Responding To Fear

The role of the brain becomes primary when the body senses danger. The nervous system gets activated and the brain sends a signal to the rest of our body. The symptoms of fear are thus experienced by the body, which include- an increase in blood pressure, rapid breathing, faster heartbeat and piloerection, also called horripilation. Blood pumps into our muscles to prepare  the body for physical action. The skin stars sweating in order to raise the body temperature. People often experience shivering in different parts of the body such as legs, hands, fingers, etc.

The body prepares itself either for a fight or flight, which means a person either fights back or runs away and avoids the situation.

If the body decides to go into flight mode, it keeps running until the brain receives the message of "being safe".

CLAUSTROPHOBIA: IS THERE AN ESCAPE?

Have you heard or experienced the fear of closed spaces, also known as claustrophobia?

Many people fear getting into an elevator, not because the elevator will crash, but because they fear getting "stuck". Some people also fear closing their bedroom doors in the dark.

Why would a closed space be so frightening? There are three reasons to it:

First, our ancient ancestors who lived in caves realized that caves are not safe. Imagine you are huddled in a cave at night and suddenly hear the call of the wild outside-wolves howling. Back then, it was very easy for wolves or tigers to go inside the cave and kill us. The caves were thus seen as dangerous, hence, the fear of closed spaces.

Second, a closed space often means 'no means to escape'. It makes us vulnerable to attack by predators and by other humans, a reason why people with agoraphobia are always looking for an exit. When they sit in a movie theatre, they want to sit at the aisle seat and as close to exit as possible. "I want to be able to get out quickly" is the sole thought running in their head.

Third, many of us with a fear of closed spaces feel that we won't be able to breathe. We fear that spaces that are closed can cut off air and suffocate us, a reason why people who panic and have agoraphobia hyperventilate. Their brain is telling them that they will suffocate, so, they gasp for air.

INTERESTING FACT

If the fear is due to a known reason and the danger Is not real, the brain may misinterpret it and can trigger unexpected response (in case you are alone in lift and electricity is gone). This happens because our brain reacts faster to danger than our ability to think and recognize what is happening. Though, once the brain adapts to the new information and accepts that there is no jeopardy, its initial response is reversed.

Can you recollect the feeling of fear?

You must have reacted to it in one of the following manners:

- Fight
- Flight
- Freeze

These are common rejoinders in living beings. These rejoinders may help you often. But sometimes stop you from performing your best. If we can recognize these three key responses to fear, we shall be equipped to handle the situation in a much better manner.

Here are a few situations which suggest a fight-flight-freeze response to fear:

- Confronting a growling dog while walking on an empty road
- Jumping out of the way of a fast-approaching vehicle
- Feeling anxious while walking down a secluded street at night

The fight-flight-freeze response is an instinctive reaction to jeopardy to protect us form an anticipated danger. This survival instinct is a gift from our ancestors. It immediately causes hormonal and physiological variation in the body, which allows the body to act instantly and protect itself.

In fight or flight response, the brain gets inactive and enters a defensive mode. The heart rate and blood pressure increases. Further, the flow of oxygen increases as the body pumps more blood into the muscles. Plight perception drops and hearing ability sharpens. These changes are very rapid and accurately executed.

On the other side, a freeze response is 'fight-or-flight on hold'. Here, you prepare to protect yourself. It is also called reactive immobility or attentive immobility. It involves similar physiological changes, but in this, you stay completely still and prepare yourself for the next move.

Fight-flight-freeze is not a conscious decision. It is an automatic reaction of your brain and body and cannot be controlled.

- To fight is to confront the threat in a crude manner
- Flight means running away from the jeopardy
- Freeze means being unable to move or act against the threat
- Fawn means to comply with the attacker to save yourself

Fight

The fight response occurs when we believe that we can knock the danger out. This is when the brain sends information to the body to prepare immediately for a physical fight. Some of its symptoms include:

- Crying
- Grinding teeth
- Speaking in a loud voice
- Experiencing intense anger
- Attempting suicide

Flight

Your brain prepares your body for flight when you are determined to run away. Running away is a smart option unless you can fight the danger. The emotional and physical reaction in flight mode includes:

- Legs become restless
- Feeling of numbness in extremities
- Eyes dilate and dart around
- You are tense
- Feeling of being trapped

Freeze

It is better to freeze if the options of fighting and flying are not viable, such as in case of a flood. Emotions and physical response during a freeze situation include:

- Feeling cold
- Numbness in your body
- Feeling of stiffness or heaviness
- An engulfing sense of dread
- Heart pounding

Fawn

A person with low self-esteem and low determination will choose fawn as an apt response to fear. Such people accept whatever they are told and do not have the courage to speak for themselves.

For example, a girl in a village who has no right to education does not have a strong will power to fight for her rights. She will easily give in to people around her and her destiny.

How does our body respond to fear?

(a) Head

You will hyperventilate and become anxious. You will experience lack of oxygen and an increase in the volume of the respiratory system due to an increase in the respiratory rate. But don't worry, it is not life-threatening. It occurs because the body tries to get more oxygen and blood in the large muscles to fight-flight-freeze.

(b) Eyes

It could make things brighter or fuzzier. You might experience black spots or some other visual effects.

(c) Fingers

When jeopardy triggers, blood starts flowing from fingers to bigger muscles, like biceps, as they would now need the energy to fight and flight. Fingers can become cold and numb as blood circulates from them.

(d) Arm Muscles

Arms muscles get afflicted to strike out the jeopardy. The body gets tensed and gets ready to face the danger head-on.

(e) Sweat Glands

The body starts working hard to get rid of the danger. A lot of energy is burnt to heat the body. So, the sweat glands work hard and secrete sweat from underarms or forehead to cool down the body.

(f) Heart

The body makes sure that blood and oxygen are pumped to major muscles such as the biceps or thighs, when the body starts preparing itself for action. This provides energy and power to strike out the jeopardy or to run as fast as possible.

(g) Stomach

When the body recognizes danger, it puts all its resources to safeguard you. The digestive system slows down as it saps all its resources and power to protect you from risk. Your brain feels that safeguarding you at the time of risk is more urgent than keeping your digestion normal. Your stomach may get upset or sore afterwards but, at that time, saving you from crisis is more important for the brain.

(h) Thigh Muscles

The muscles are forced to run away or fight back to cope with the jeopardy. At the time of peril, the body becomes stressed and readies itself to be in motion.

What happens inside the brain?

Fear begins inside the brain.

We do not have to think about breathing, digesting food, or making our heart beat. The nervous system takes care of these functions automatically. This is because our nervous system is divided into two branches: the parasympathetic nervous system (the rest and digest system) and the sympathetic nervous system (the fight-or-flight system).

Fear kicks the fight-or-flight response into overdrive. Adrenal glands secrete adrenaline. Blood flow decreases to the brain's frontal lobe, which is responsible for logical thinking and planning, and the deeper, more animalistic parts of the brain—including the amygdala—take over. Cortisol, the stress hormone, helps the brain to think clearly, sends energy to vital muscles, and increases heart rate and breathing.

In this situation, all the body's resources get pushed toward one goal-staying alive.

Just imagine what would happen if we are face-to-face with a bear. Will these body functions caused by the release of Cortisol be of use then?

Of course, yes!

When confronted by a bear, we will have to think about how to rescue ourselves. We need to use our muscles to run faster; need to have a faster heartbeat to pump more blood to the muscles; and faster breath rate to inhale more oxygen. To ensure all this and in order to overcome stress, our brain will release two hormones—Cortisol and Adrenaline.

How does brain cope up with imaginary fear?

It is important to understand that our experience of danger is more psychological or social in nature as the brain does not know how to differentiate between real danger and perceived danger. It simply tends to work on the command we give. It means that along with reacting to real life-threatening situations like a car crash or any natural calamity, the brain can also react to situations like stress at workplace as it perceives it as real danger. Our feeling of anxiety is an emotional kickback to situations like these where the brain perceives the situation to be a threat, but actually it is not.

Often, this anxiety can be good as it commands the brain and body about an upcoming threat that needs to be avoided or ignored. For instance, being late at work will not kill you but it could cost you your job and feeling anxious about it can help you reach there on time. Similarly, going out late at night might not necessarily mean a threat but the fear within guides you to go out with a friend and avoid an unfavourable situation.

Our physical reaction to anxiety is equivalent to that of fear, but generally to a lesser extent. A panic attack, on the other hand, is a "pure fight-or-flight reaction."

Now that we know how our body reacts to fear, let us talk about the hormones responsible behind them and under what circumstances do they get triggered.

Stress hormones

Remember how your body reacts when you receive a message from your boss at an unofficial hour? Doesn't it feel like there is a lion on the loose? Soulful gratitude to the work of our sympathetic nervous system—the "fight or flight" system—that takes over when we are stressed. Here are the hormones that add fuel to fire during those times.

(a) Adrenaline

Adrenaline is famously known as the fight or flight hormone. When you are in a stressful situation, your brain signals the Adrenal Glands to release Adrenaline, which along with Norepinephrine, responds immediately to the situation.

Just imagine a situation when you are subconsciously crossing the road, without being aware of the surroundings. The consciousness returns when you are at the middle of the road, about to bump into a vehicle. Immediately, your heart starts pounding, your muscles get stressed, you start sweating and run as fast as possible to arrive at a safe spot.

Your Adrenaline saved you. Along with the increase in heart rate, Adrenaline also gives you a surge of energy which helps you to run away from the peril, and bring your focus back to the present situation.

(b) Norepinephrine

The primary responsibility of Norepinephrine, like Adrenaline, is arousal. In a stressful situation, it helps you to become more responsible and attentive. Norepinephrine helps in shifting blood from areas where it is not crucial (such as skin) towards your muscles so that you can flee the stressful scenario.

(c) Cortisol

Cortisol, steroid hormone, also known as stress hormone- is transported through the bloodstream to the cells of various target organs where it regulates a wide range of physiological functions. Cortisol takes more time to respond minutes, rather than seconds.

The release of this hormone kicks in a multi-step process, engaging two additional minor hormones.

Foremost, Amygdala, a crucial part of the brain admits the presence of a threat. Thereafter, it signals the Hypothalamus (a part of brain) to release Corticotropin- releasing Hormone (CRH). CRH then tells the Pituitary Gland to release the Adrenocorticotropic Hormone (ACTH), which in turn asks the Adrenal Glands to produce Cortisol.

When we are in survival mode, the optimal amount of Cortisol is life-saving. It helps in maintaining fluid balance and blood pressure while readjusting some inessential body functions at that moment, like immunity, digestion, reproductive drive, and growth.

But if we are constantly in a stressful situation, the prolonged release of Cortisol can lead to serious issues within our body. Excessive Cortisol can curb the immune system, increase blood pressure and sugar, decrease libido, produce acne, contribute to obesity, and more.

(d) Other hormones

Oestrogen and Testosterone are other hormones that affect our reaction to stress, as are the neurotransmitters Dopamine and Serotonin. However, the classic fight- or-flight reaction is majorly due to the three big players mentioned above.

You may fight-flight-freeze-fawn, depending on the situation. But never forget that you have just one life. So do not live it like you are living in a cyclone. Live every moment blissfully and stay joyful.

6

Fear Is Good

Fear is natural. We all feel it in our gut at some point or the other. But do you know that the anxious feeling which keeps you at our wits' end can actually be good for you? Yes, fear can be our guiding star in keeping us away from dangerous situations and prompting us to not go too far. It is one of the most crucial emotions for our survival.

How many times have you felt extremely uncomfortable while daring to do something that is outside your comfort zone or smells a bit uncertain? When it tells you "Hey there! I know that you are trying to challenge yourself but is it truly worth entertaining all that anxiety and risk? Should you actually be pushing that far?"

It is in moments like this when fear is communicating with you, and trying to protect you against something that might not be of benefit to you. At this point, if fear is making you uncomfortable, it is actually protecting you from landing into a physical or emotional stress. It is befriending you. And, there is

no need to fight with it just to prove yourself. All that you need to do is 'be with it, understand it and follow where it leads you'.

Certainly, we are not fighting wars or being faced by a wild animal like our predecessors did. But, even today, fear can get us out of the most threatening situations. For, when real danger looms and our body is gripped by fear, we are our most intuitive self. Fear blurs rational thinking and makes us act fast on our instincts, just like our ancestors acted when attacked by wild animals. Fear helps us to stay out of harm's way.

Having said that, certain fears can and should be transcended. Because, when you overcome them, you push yourself into the next orbit of growth. Ever saw a baby trying to take his first steps? He tries to get up and walk, countless times, only to fall back to the ground. But the fear of falling back, the fear of failing yet again, is incapable of holding him back. He tries, tries and tries again, until he is finally able to take his first few steps and announce his victory over his fears. Similarly, at times, it is good to dive into the ocean of fears, challenge them and rise above. Just listen to your inner voice, and you will know which ones are worth transcending.

Here is a list of the benefits that fear brings with itself, and will encourage you to fight yours.

The benefits of fear

(a) Fear keeps you protected

Fear acts as an alert. It compels us to take action carefully, and helps us to make sensible and vigilant decisions. Without fear, we may not live very long as we wouldn't be protecting ourselves against the risks around us.

Take a mother and child for instance. When a child tries to put his fingers in the electrical socket for the first time, the fear in the mother compels her to close the socket with tapes, thus protecting her child. Similarly, a dog might propel towards you, and the absence of fear might render you incapable of reacting in that split second. When you get scared, your brain gives signals to your body to react physically and handle the jeopardy, also called the fight-or-flight response. Without this fear response, you wouldn't have the energy, focus, speed or strength to fight or flee.

(b) Fear as challenge

A person with a steady job but deeply inclined towards business is challenged by his fear of losing his fixed monthly income and failing in his business. Unless he transcends this challenge, he would never be able to become a flourishing businessman, and realize his true potential.

Fear challenges us to take the leap and create new experiences. And, unless you overcome it, you would not know what lies at the other end. If you let fear enclose you, it will suck you into a negative spiral and never let you succeed. Fear feeds upon itself. The more you resist fear, the stronger it becomes, and more challenging it becomes to act. If you desire an extraordinary experience, but are scared of the possible slip-ups which may happen along the process, you are losing and fear is winning the competition. Let's learn to move faster than your fear. Success is about risk taking and making strong decisions.

(c) Fear as motivation

Remember that feeling a fortnight before University exams? How scared were you because you had not prepared well? And how that fear motivated you to work harder and prepare better for success!

Be open to the emotion of fear, let it settle and find your way back to rational thoughts. Once emotionally in control, use fear as your motivator and coach, to push you through challenging situations. As you prove fear wrong over and over again, you develop the character trait of confidence. Without fear, confidence cannot develop. You become confident through continually and successfully achieving things which you never before thought that you were capable of doing or achieving. When used correctly, fear will drive you harder towards success than any other emotion.

(d) Fear as snoopiness

What happens when you watch a horror film for the first time? You are scared. But, are you still scared watching it for the second time? Why not? This is because now the suspense is over. You know the secret and have come to terms with it.

Now think about it in real life. Are you scared of heights? Or the dark, anger, water, loneliness? A past instance might have nurtured this feeling of fear within you. Try looking for it. Once you will find the answer, you will no longer be scared. Fear does not appear without reason.

In business, thoughts of failure or loss naturally lead us to do anything that we can to avoid these experiences. However, avoidance does not serve any purpose. Instead, it breaks down our creativity and creates mental blocks, which in turn curbs success.

If you do not wish to become a prey to your own fear, be in snoopiness about what you are scared of. Being mentally aware of your fears gives you the opportunity to find answers to what needs to be done to fight this negative mindset, and use that energy in the right direction for your own benefit.

(e) Fear as mentor

What happens when a child falls down from a height? He gets scared of repeating the act. But, in the event, he learns to play it safer the next time. Now, he would assess his surroundings, evaluate the heights, look at his options, and probably place some cushions underneath to not hurt himself when he jumps next.

Fear puts you in an autopilot state, enforcing you to be attentive when handling challenges in life. Fear alarms you when to be cautious and when to be bold in decision making. Listen to its voice. There are times when fear will indicate you "it is now or never," and other times when it will indicate you "rest on it, grant it time." These are your play cards to negotiate and plan your next stride.

(f) Fear is valuable

The best fruits anyone ever ate are the ones plucked from the tree. But it involved the fear of climbing the height, falling down a few times, hurting yourself, before you could actually make it there, and taste the forbidden fruit. Whether you take falling as a negative experience (fear) or use it to climb better the next time decides whether you will get to taste the fruit or not.

Fear isn't good or bad. When you give fear the incoherent power to demolish you, it will squelch your progress. As you engage with fear as an opportunity (a positive experience), it will be an asset which will drive your self-evolution and career growth. As you practice to go beyond fear, you learn to respect fear as the gateway to your greatest success, happiness and contentment.

Therefore, always remember everything you want stands on the other side of fear.

(g) Fear as a mentor

Fear is closely tied to viscera instinct. Though this emotion can feel uneasy, it provides for the tough-love, which you generally do not accept graciously from others. When your thoughts and emotions get the best of you, you are forced to listen. If you want to use fear efficiently, snip the direction of your emotional state towards wisdom, and break the threshold of your comfort zone. Mastering fearful emotions can become the most powerful mentor that can guide you for your personal and business decisions.

(h) Fear as a catalyst

Never let the fear of social acceptance get the better of you. Be authentic and transparent. These are virtues, just like a magnet, that attracts success. The less fearful you are about being different, you will find more opportunities travelling your way. Allow yourself to take risks. Be vulnerable. Learn to make something magical out of this powerful emotion.

Fear is a catalyst. Let it drive you to your complete potential.

(i) Feeling fear is feeling alive

Feeling fear, in the right dose, is fun and exciting.

People like me scare themselves deliberately—and not just around Halloween but also by riding roller coasters, climbing mountains, experiencing wildlife, skydiving or sailing through notorious white-water rapids.

Leaving the comfort zone is where fear starts. Though, it also gives a feeling of liveliness, full of adventure and fun. This liveliness can evaporate your stress and depression by increasing Adrenaline, which helps in increased arousal, excitement and a glucose splurge (converted into energy).

(j) Fear is empowering

Fear gives you the power to enhance your self-esteem. There's a good reason for that. When we experience fear, chemicals such as dopamine, endorphins, oxytocin, serotonin and adrenaline are released in our body which helps our brain to work more efficiently and boosts our energy.

How does that happen? Let me explain through an example.

Sachin Tendulkar was the first player to hit a double century. Until then everyone used to believe that it may not be possible. With this new record, Sachin had set a new benchmark which challenged other players. Now, they were in fear and pressure to perform and break the new record. In turn, they became more focused.

Like these players, every human brain craves for new challenges. It is the key to neuroplasticity. So, every time we face a challenge and accomplish our goals, we feel self-empowered. This natural high booster dose of energy often lasts longer than the time we spend in feeling scared, which is why we feel so great afterward.

As Ralph Waldo Emerson said "Do the thing, and you will have the power," which means that the moment we decide to do something that scares us, we have already generated the higher energy that we need to accomplish it.

(k) Fear keeps us in the present moment and help us stay focused

My friend was extremely scared of water. But, seeing her daughter slipping into the sea, she decided to dive in. The fear of losing her daughter in the water helped her to forget her own fears, be in the moment and stay focussed, till she finally could find the little girl and make her way out. Today, she has learnt to swim and is teaching her daughter too.

We spend most of our lives thinking about the future. The uncertainties in life, including financial issues, always tend to scare us. Here we have two options, (a) either we keep worrying and getting anxious and fearful, or (b) grab the opportunity, make ourselves more focused, add more skills which can enhance our financial condition and make us a better person.

As we discussed above, adrenaline is released when we are scared, which alerts our nervous system to get into gear. Norepinephrine, another hormone, is released by fear to keep us focussed instead of getting panicked. Norepinephrine allows clearer thinking under stress, which is why it's used in many antidepressants. Together, these fear hormones help us to live in now and take better decisions in life.

(l) Fear helps us bond

When the feeling of fear is released, Oxytocin is activated. This hormone is associated with pro-social behaviour. Oxytocin makes us comfortable in socialising with others.

(m) Fear gives us clarity about our priorities

When we're fearful for a sick mother in the house, an injured leg or a career plan; our fear can become an opportunity to clarify and take care of what is truly most vital and a priority in our life. Very often we keep saying to ourselves: "if I have more time, I'll spend it with my family, pursue my passion, travel the world or explore more"? Fear makes us realize that "now" is the only time when we can achieve and follow through our dreams. "Later" is never guaranteed.

Today, when I am writing this book, the whole world is being challenged by the Coronavirus pandemic. The whole world is locked down and facing an economic crisis. Everyone is in fear. But those who have clarity are taking this fear and lockdown as an opportunity to spend time with family, enhance skills and do whatever they love to do.

The Sweat Blot of Fear

The day when fear meets courage is the sweat blot in which mountains are scaled and oceans are navigated. Above all the things, fear can be the mother of change, creativity, exploration and innovation. Let's embrace our fear. Not the real fears that are life-threatening, but the ones that come in tiny bites. A tiny bit of fear is for our best, and transforms us into a value-added version of ourselves.

In conclusion, fear itself isn't a jeopardy. Our reaction to it is the problem. In making fear an antagonist, we forget the message hidden in it that is being sent to us by the universe, a lesson to make us a better person. When we choose to make it an ally, we achieve more than we expect. If you are standing in front of a door that says "fear", that is the very door you must walk through to become successful.

As the old adage goes, 'success begins right outside your comfort zone'. There is no fear in comfort. There is nothing driving you when there is security. Where there is comfort, there is complacency. Complacency is the greatest counterforce to success. To become abundantly successful you must master fear, understand its true purpose and use it to your greatest advantage. When you know fear and how to use it, you will actualize your success.

7

In Confrontation With Fear

What do we normally do with our fear?

Mostly we don't want to face them. We sow our fear deep inside ourselves or push it away. What we do not know is that 'when we persist to resist our fear, it becomes stronger'.

Let me explain this through an example.

A girl got up one night, brimming with fear, submerged in panic. Fear was dashing through her veins. Her mind and heart were on a roller coaster ride. She was completely frozen. She started thinking– "What is troubling me? What am I thinking? Is it the fear of failure? Is it something else? Who will hold me if I collapse? Why is my heart beating so erratically?" She crossed her finger and wished for things to calm down. It did not.

Finally, she turned on the light, thinking that it will help her to chase her fear. Then she picked up a book to read, thinking that doing this will divert her mind from fear. She read a sentence, again, then again, and repeated it a thousand times. But she failed distracting herself from her thoughts. Eventually, she felt asleep till the alarm rang. Though, as she woke up, her fear remained attached to her and kept lingering tightly throughout the day.

How could she release this fear? What could she do? The answer lies in confronting her fears.

Expose yourself to fear

If fear is the reason behind your sufferings it is because you have not exposed yourself to it yet. The day you stop running away from fear, fear will stop chasing you. Dare to approach fear, with confidence and determination. Do not show it your back. Do not bother what other people would think about you if they come to know about your fear. Do not worry about their scorns that make you feel vulnerable.

Accept and acknowledge fear and vulnerability as a vital part of yourself. Get into the mode of self-acceptance. Doing this will help you to feel light, remain light, and spread light. This will also help you to nurture and accept your loved ones just as they are and help them to overcome their fears.

True, facing your fears will not be easy. You might have to confront them again and again before they are gone. For instance, if you are anxious about flying in airplanes since your childhood, the anxiety cannot go immediately, when you try flying at the age of 40. It may take years for you to overcome it. But once you spot your fear and are determined to overcome it, the anxiety around it will certainly start reducing.

When faced by a fear, don't ask what to do, instead ask, what not to do?

You have to do nothing to release your own fears. Fear- the problem that we have created for ourselves can vanish if we pause to fight with it.

Though there are multiple ways to reduce or overcome it but acceptance is first and foremost. Just witness your response and whatsoever comes your way. Remain light, be light, and let it go. It will go if you allow it to go. And you will shine bright and pure with a child-like innocence.

Let fear be the way it is. Do not do anything about it. Allow it to take you far. Once it takes you far and abandons you, you can know for sure that the fear has departed. You will now feel focused and free, as you never felt before. Once you have mastered the art of letting it be, you will have the master key which unlocks the doors to your inner self. After that, whatsoever the situation is, let it be. Be a detached witness and let it be, the way it is. Allow whatever happens to happen.

Accept that fear has to be faced to make it disappear. Agony has to be crossed before it is gone. The more accurate is the confrontation, the more you face it with determination and confidence, the more you accept it as it is, the faster your fear will abandon you.

However, the effectiveness of this process, from the acceptance of fear and letting it be to its disappearance, would depend upon your authenticity and your intensity. It might take much time—five days, five years, or five lives- depending upon your intention and your vibrations. Five seconds can work in case you have the courage to go through the purgatory with a high intensity, something which might tear you apart and become unbearable. If you are ready to face the negative hidden within your inner self, fear shall pass.

Break your thresholds. Choose to experience fear

"Being brave isn't the absence of fear. Being brave is having that fear but finding a way through it".

All of us must have, at some point, faced and experienced our worst fear, something that we were not ready for. Nonetheless, if we do not acknowledge and face this fear, it will control and drive our behaviour negatively and will make us suffer.

Most fears arise due to our own decisions—the difficult and risky choices that we have to make in our lives to rise and succeed. The bigger the opportunity and scope of growth, the higher is the challenge and tougher is the choice we make. These decisions make us uneasy as they push us to break our thresholds.

If you have taken such a decision based on your sensibilities and valid rationales, do not let the fear that arises from it make you step back. Be determined and stick to that decision. However, if the decision is a casual one, particularly made in a stressful state of mind, it would be best to think twice, and reverse it instead of fighting with your fears.

Fear creates negative thoughts

Fear is negative energy which is later converted into thoughts. When these thoughts are repeated simultaneously in our subconscious, they become our reality. Once fear starts guiding our reality, it starts driving our mood and behaviour. We start becoming prisoners to it. Fear, if not channelized assertively, can ruin our life to a large extent.

Your responsibility thus lies in being conscious about the thought that you create and the stories that you share. Do you really want to live these stories in real life? If not, create something which empowers you and the people around you.

Once you realize that you have the power to change your own thoughts and their frequency from a lower level to a higher level, it would feel like a miracle. You would have control on your destiny. And you will feel empowered.

Just imagine! With this power, you have the power to become calm, creative, or anything else that you may want. You will be able to design your life just as you desire. You will become the master creator of your thoughts.

8

Fear v/s Relationships

*F*ew years ago, a person visited me to be healed. He was 34 years old and was in the phase of building his career. He came to me directly from his office and I could hear him shouting at someone on a call, just before he entered my room.

As he entered, he said: "Hi ma'am!" (smile on face but anxiety in the brain).

I asked: "Are you alright?." He nodded.

I offered him a glass of water and asked him to calm down. His anger calmed a bit and he narrated his story.

The work overload was keeping him busy and he often got late while returning home. Eventually, his wife had begun to doubt him. Regular fights between them had become a norm at his residence. Though, this so-called normal was having a mental impact on their child. Then, one fine day, his wife asked for a divorce. This was why he had come to me.

I explained the fear behind his wife's behaviour. She had the fear and insecurity of losing him. Though, the fear was not real.

Within a few sessions with him and his wife, their problem was resolved. Today, they are living happily with their son.

Like this man, how many of us are trapped in this dirty dust of fear?

Just think!

I deal so much with it. Couples quarrel due to frivolous issues and never actually try to address the underlying reasons for their unhappiness. They hide away from their fears and beat around the bush, further aggravating their fears and insecurities.

It has been universally found that most women have a core fear of disconnection – they fear not being listened to, not being valued, somehow losing the love of their loved ones.

Maximum men, on the other side, have a fear of helplessness or getting controlled–they fear failure or getting tiptoed.

The core fears are related to two primary fears: the fear of being controlled (losing power) and the fear of being disconnected (separation from people and being alone). Until you identify your own core fear and understand how you tend to react when you are in fear, your relationships will keep suffering.

In a particular case of husband-wife relationship, the couple fought daily since the wife feared that her husband was cheating on her while the husband had no clue of how his wife was feeling and the fear that she was dealing with. In reality, the wife conceived this fear when she was much younger and used to see her father coming late from work very frequently. Later, the family found out that this was because her father was seeing another woman. The fear of a woman being deceived by a man thus got etched in her subconscious, which she was now transmuting into her own reality. While she and her husband argued continuously, her fear did not surface until much later.

Couples who are dealing with this fear know the steps well.

- The play begins with a feeling of heartache or anxiety.

- You desperately want to stop experiencing the emotional turmoil and want the other person to stop treating you in this manner.

- You wish your partner to change. So, you overreact.

- Eventually, it becomes a part of your habit and you start the same process over with another person.

The fear can start with discussions about rights and space in relationships, money, in-laws, being late, etc. When our brain hits the fear button, we start falling into patterns of reacting. In most cases, people choose unhealthy reactions to pact with fear. In order to make ourselves feel better, we use different mechanisms to bring a transition in the other person's lifestyle and behaviour. The end result—our relationships are ruined.

Types of fear in a relationship

(a) Fear of being left alone

We experience this when we fear that our loved ones would leave us and go. Thus, we act aggressively and provoke them, consciously or unconsciously, to test our relationships and feel secured.

(b) Fear of getting hurt

Trusting people is our core characteristic since childhood. However, in some cases, we are unable to nurture this trust amongst our relationships. For instance, a soldier is always conditioned to distrust his opponent. This also impacts his relationship as he is always in doubt and fears getting hurt by his partner, should he choose to trust her.

(c) Fear of not getting emotional support or attention

When we experience lack of attention, understanding, and emotional support, we start feeling emotionally deprived. This creates a fear of loneliness. Thoughts like, "they don't love me, "I don't have anyone who loves me" and "no one cares for me," keep doing rounds in our mind and gives birth to a continuous sense of fear.

Likewise, many people think that they are not good enough to deserve someone. They demean and belittle themselves. Their thoughts roll around: "they may reject me", "they are better looking", "I do not match their standards" etc. People with this fear hide their feelings and their true self. They always compare themselves with others and cannot handle criticism.

(d) Fear of getting rejected due to failure

The fear of failure is the biggest fear that can ruin any relationship. People living with this fear allow others to criticize and demoralize them and subconsciously hide their potential from other.

Did any of these fears ring a bell?

If yes, let's read further on how to deal with these fears:

- First thing first, you need to work on yourself. You can't change others. Therefore, identify the situation which triggers your brain and creates fear. Be in awareness about the negative thoughts which place you in such a situation.

- Hang a mirror and look back in the past to identify the actual incident that triggered this fear in you, and understand how profound is its impact on you. This will help you be aware and mindful of your reaction when the same situation gets repeated.

- Led by fear, when you feel yourself losing control, do not react immediately. Hold on, take a deep breath, and pause only when you find yourself in the present moment. Doing this will ensure that you do not operate from your past and make the same mistakes when you are in fear.

- Disappear for a moment from the place of argument if you can't control your reaction. Now, try to come back to the present moment and let go of the immediate past. This is how you will be able to respond, not react. It will save from causing harm to your current relationship.

Now that we have spoken about what may affect a couple relationship, and how to overcome the related fears, let us focus on the reasons for fear at workplace, how they impact relationships with boss, peers and juniors, and how to deal with it.

Types of fear at workplace

(a) Fear of failure at work

If everyone was perfect, the world would have been an ideal place. But it is not like that. So, failure is not bad or abnormal.

79

It is a part of life and we should not run from it. There are many examples in history that have proved that failure is not bad. Many legends are born after failure.

I once met the CEO of a company and he told me that they purposefully created various scenarios for failures. He said that they believe to failure is an excellent mentor that teaches people to learn and grow. He emphasized that it is how the organization trains its people to respond appropriately to failure.

It is not employees who are responsible for their fear of failure; the responsibility lies with their managers. While assigning any task to an individual, a manager should ask himself if he is assigning the right task to the right employee or not? Is the employee to whom the task is being assigned overburdened?

The employees should be able to communicate freely to ensure that there is no communication gap. A manager should ensure that, for his people, failure should be a reason to grow and learn, and not a reason to experience fear.

(b) Fear of Embarrassment

Embarrassment at the workplace is a foot-in-mouth moment for anyone. No one wants to get embarrassed on intention, specifically in front of their juniors and colleagues. For instance, why would someone intentionally mark a copy of the mail to the wrong person when he knows how embarrassing and job risking it may be? Recovering from embarrassment can be impossible for some people, and push them to take serious actions, including suicide.

On the flip side, studies have shown that embarrassment can be positive and can lead to a positive action at work. A manager can just let an embarrassing moment pass instead of making an issue of it. This can help him to build trust with his employees and make his employees comfortable in his company. The embarrassing moment can thus become a learning and growing experience for people and the organization, if handled sensibly.

(c) Fear of Underperformance

Performance at workplace can always be subjective. It is always possible for an employee to be a pro-performer in comparison to others. But it is important for the manager to know how the other employees feel about this. Is it making them worried, and giving them a sense of being underperformers? Is it pushing them to work extra hours and on weekends?

It is the responsibility of a manager to ensure that all employees feel confident and comfortable while taking charge of a new project. It is crucial to have realistic expectations and be communicable. Most often, when expectations are not communicated, employees underperform and are unable to unleash their true potential, and develop a fear of underperformance.

(d) Fear of Rejection

People with a fear of rejection generally resist to put their views in front of their boss. The fear forces them to undervalue their own opinions, ideas and work. In such a scenario, the manager should cheer the employee, motivate him, build his confidence and make him comfortable about sharing his opinions. Managers should stop being biased and play favouritism in office. It is on them to provide equal opportunity to every employee, and help them in realizing their qualities and potential.

(e) Fear of Change and Uncertainty

Technology is changing every day. This makes the need to change obvious at workplace. However, employees resist this change and wish to remain in their comfort zone– the older zone. The continuously changing technological landscape, and culture within offices, creates a sense of uncertainty within the employees, and gives birth to the fear of change and the uncertainties that may arise from it in the future.

Communication and transparency are the best solutions to handle this fear of change and uncertainty. The managers should be transparent with the employees, and keep them in loop about the changes that are expected in the future. They should be given the responsibility to hold periodic trainings on the significance and impact of change on the organization and the roles and responsibilities of its employees. Every employee should have the freedom to raise questions about the future uncertainties, which should be answered humbly.

(f) Fear of Confrontation

Employees feel offensive and develop negative emotions if they are confronted openly in front of their peers. Doing this hurts their self-respect.

The manager has to thus ensure that no employee is confronted in front of their peers or in open. Office confrontations should always be in private. The managers should also bring the employee in confidence and gain his trust before pulling him aside for an uneasy talk.

Quick Recap

Let us do a quick recap of what you can do to control your fear and create harmony in your relationships:

- Think before you speak—Your thoughts determine your feelings and actions. Control them if you feel that they can hurt someone.

- Take charge of your fear buttons: Know how to react when someone pushes your fear button.

- Don't allow others to control your feelings: Deny focusing on what the other person has said or done. You can just change yourself, not others.

- Don't expect others to make you feel good: Don't fall into the "If you scratch my back, I'll scratch yours" myth. You are responsible for your own happiness. Do not depend on others to make you feel happy.

- Become the boss of your life: Be careful about expressing your expectations to others for doing this can let them inside your personal space and give them the power to control you.

- Forgive them to heal your relationships: Sometimes it is not even your fault but it is still for your own good to say sorry and forgive them for what they have done.

9

Live In The Moment

*"Live in now to give yourself the gift
of eternal peace and happiness."*

When we start to live in the present, the now moment, peace, and happiness flow willingly into our life. Acceptance of the present moment ends all fears and anxieties.

In the context of the Bhagawad Gita, it is written "whatever is happening is true! Accept it as it is!

It seems like an eternity now, but when I started my practice, I experimented on this concept.

It was 10:00 AM, Monday, my first day on job, and I was already late.

I felt threatened and my fight or flight response started to kick in. I wanted to run away. But I didn't. Rather, I took a deep breath, walked to my desk, and took another long deep breath. Inhale... exhale... inhale... exhale.

I praised my job and released my ego, slowly coming into the present moment. Thereafter, when things went flat, I trusted the flow. When things fell apart, I trusted the flow. When I made mistakes, I trusted the flow. So did I while finding the solution.

I used my all determination, put tremendous efforts and released my attachment with the outcome.

Eventually, everything around me seemed to blossom. Not only did I stop feeling fearful of losing my job, but within a few months, I was promoted to a leadership role.

Were things perfect? Absolutely Not!

But the moment I changed my perception, it caused a ripple effect that changed my thought process and actions. As a result, everything changed around me and my reality started shaping up just as I wanted it to be.

The culture and people did not change overnight, but as I let go of my self-resistance, the challenges I faced in my environment vanished. And, I learnt that embracing struggle is the end of fear.

Running away from circumstances is like running away from a mirror. You do it since you do not like to see the reflection that the mirror shows you. The reality of fear and stress is very well visible on your face. You may try to hide or run to a different mirror (and keep changing it) but you will continue to see the same reflection until you accept and change the reality of life, and transform it into that of peace and happiness.

Change in our external environment will not happen until we change ourselves from within. The fearful situation will continue to dominate us if we resist and try to escape from the present moment.

Instead of escaping, grab every moment as an opportunity, especially the unfavourable ones that can help you to practice the art of being in the present moment. Living in the moment is a habit. The habit can become a characteristic and characteristics can become a lifestyle if you practice them regularly.

Practice letting go

Let go of your resistance. It will put you in a state of flow.

Understand it like this. The moments in our life are like waves in the ocean. When we accept the present moment, these waves, inevitably guide us to our higher purpose. Once we reach the destination and look back, we feel grateful for all the challenges that came our way and created circumstances that helped us to align ourselves with our intention and purpose.

Be in the present to overcome fear and anxiety

A research shows that the majority of people either live in the past or future. We keep looking for the next moment or the one gone by rather than appreciating the present one.

Take a pause from your fast-moving life and ask yourself these questions:

- What if I don't wake up the next morning?
- What if I die next moment?
- Would I like to die with a lot of anxiety and negativity?

Thinking about these helped me to live in the present moment.

Truth be told, all we have is the present moment. We do not know what the next moment holds. We don't even know if the next moment exists. So, why to spoil this moment in fear and anxiety when we can choose to be happy and peaceful?

> *"Doing the best at this moment puts you in the best place for the next moment."*
>
> *–Oprah Winfrey*

Using Present for a better life

Become mindful and be present in the body by reminding yourself that you are just a soul playing your role on this earth. Your part is accurate. You were supposed to do what you are doing. Universe has its own plans for you. Believing in this will transform your thought process and pull you from negativity towards positivity.

"The accuracy of your focus and attention on the present moment will determine your future."

In Mahabharata when Shri Krishan asked Arjuna "what are you focusing on? What are you able to see, what is your goal?

Arjuna replied, "I am able to see only fish, which is my target."

Have you ever thought deeply about Arjuna's reply? Why did he say that?

Because, he was in the present moment. He was able to

achieve his goal as he was focused only at the present moment.

Fear can help you stay in the present

Fear can play a vital role in helping you to stay in the present moment. Yes! Here are four things about fear that will help you to stay in the present and feel much calmer in life.

(a) Fear is often about the future

Often, our anxiety is driven by anticipation. Life brings in endless uncertainties that fuel our stress and fear. Unusually though, fear can act like an armour to such uncertainties of life, usually thrown at us like daggers. If we learn to predict or visualize our fears, we might have control over our circumstances.

I have heard many people saying that they feel protected from future uncertainties when they are fearful. It's just a huge myth we spend our life on. But when we go far ahead and realize that it was not true, we regret to have not lived in the present moment throughout.

I have seen many ladies in the villages, who in the fear of future and superstitions, conduct witchcraft on others and spread negativity. They waste their entire life in this rather than enjoying the present moment.

(b) Fear can originate from the past

It is human to store the memories of past events and recall them every now and then. This store and recall mechanism of our past memories makes it very difficult for us to forgive and forget (ourselves and others). We keep carrying our bad experiences, and regrets till death.

Though we would like to believe that our current fear about work or our present insecurities about our relationships is entirely based on our present circumstances, the ways in which we feel, react, and treat ourselves during these situations speak volumes about unresolved issues and blocked energies from our past that have been stirred in the present. A similar experience or event that must have occurred in the past is enough to trigger the emotions that we felt back then. This, in itself, is an evidence that our past has a lot to do with our current fears, and can serve as a powerful tool to overcome our fears in the present.

(c) Fear could be fired by the critical inner voice

The chaos that pushes us into the past and future comes from our critical inner voice—a self-destructive thought process that undermines and lowers our self-esteem, based on which we drive our life and live in fear.

Hence, it is vital to reconnect with the present moment. Like every coin has two sides, we also have two choices in life.

- The information from the past that we are feeding our brains with can disempower us and provoke us to spoil our life, or;

- We can use the same information to empower ourselves.

Our way of responding to our circumstances defines our maturity in handling fear. If we are ready to stop and take a deep breath, we can experience peace and happiness. You can also do it by meditating, listening to music, and giving yourself enough time and space to experience peace.

THE WORLD IS YOUR OWN REFLECTION

An angry man sat in the middle of a room filled with mirrors. He looked around and saw a hundred angry men glaring back at him. He showed them his fist and saw them showing their fist in response. Then, a small girl entered the room. Amused, she started giggling and saw a hundred girls giggling back. Soon, her giggles turned into laughter and spread across the room. Both of them got back what they reflected to the world.

We can Overcome Fear

Have you ever thought, why do we remain connected to our world of imagination, afraid of the future, or remorseful about the past? Can we stop time traveling and grant ourselves the permission to go offline—to live in the present moment and enjoy the life to fullest?

Whenever you feel yourself entering into your world of imagination, a dreaded past or a scary future, take a deep breath. Reconnect with your inner self and pay gratitude for this moment you are living in. This will help you to stop going back and forth in time, and be at peace.

You can also challenge our "critical inner voice" by checking if it is in your favour or not. The best way to do it by analysing if your thoughts are putting you in space of self-compassion or stress? Check if these thoughts are negative and unnecessary thoughts or positive and necessary thoughts. Notice the speed and direction of your thoughts. Whenever you feel that your mind is taken over by your inner critic, talk to it. Request it to come back to the present moment.

Love has a lot of power. If you love your mind and heart, they will start following you. But if you are harsh on them, the consequences will be likewise. Treat yourself kindly and with compassion. Challenge your inner critical voice by being in love with yourself, your brain, and heart so that you can win.

Gift yourself and your loved ones the gift of the present moment.

AT THE OTHER SIDE OF PANIC

Mr. Max battled chronic anxiety throughout his life.

He was well aware of the impact that dread and panic could have on his body and mind. On his good days, when he drove himself to numbness through consumption of alcohol or self-medication, he could somehow manage to get by. But, on his bad days, he could feel his chest and throat tighten as he struggled to breathe. Chronic panic attacks would leave him curled up in a foetal position.

He was not just battling anxiety; he was in denial about a low-grade, high-functioning depression that, like a dark little storm cloud, hovered over him from the time his eyes opened in the morning till he finally fell asleep at night. He tried everything possible he could to shake it off. He worked hard to blow past the inner turmoil. But, he could not.

He couldn't resist it. Neither could he make it disappear. At-least, not for a long-term. Some things he tried provided brief momentary relief, but eventually, the feeling of fear, defeat, and anxiety would grip him yet again. He felt stuck, trapped and powerless, doubtful if he would ever be able to experience anything other than this wretched existence.

He had a family history of mental disorder and addiction and believed that agony and suffering was in his blood. He told me,how, as a young child, he grew up witnessing his at her struggle with severe depression, bipolar disorder, and substance abuse, all of which eventually led to several meltdowns and multiple suicide attempts. Naturally, he was an anxious and fearful little boy who often felt very unsafe. He shared that his young mind learned too early that in order to survive, he had to be on a constant guard. His nervous system became accustomed to the constant stress-mode and was on a continuous fight-freeze-or-flight.

In order to cope up and make sense of his situation, he sought ways that could help him to feel in control of himself and his life. He thought that if he could accomplish a certain sense of control through distraction, numbing himself out, or playing small, so be it.

As we worked together, I helped him to heal and gain control on his thoughts and emotions. This is what he wrote to me on one fine day:

Dear Peyush ma'am,

I am thankful for all your help. Thank you for helping me in believing that yogic breathing works. Thank you for introducing me to this ancient practice, which taught me that I am not my past and I am not where I come from.

Thanks to the yoga practice that you taught me; it has helped me realize that my anxiety didn't have to define me. I learned that I could certainly rise above all my fears and negativity, even in the midst of a full-blown panic attack. I could learn to calm my shouting mind and hyper-aroused body by learning to inhale deep breaths.

It wasn't easy to employ these techniques in the middle of an attack, but with your help, practice, time, consistency, and dedication, my panic attacks gradually vanished. They lessened their hold on me.

I haven't had a panic attack in almost three years. Each time I'd feel the onslaught of an attack, it took everything I had in me to channel my inner yogic warrior and brace myself for the internal battle about to take place. I'd remind myself over and over again as I struggled to breathe. "I am not my fear; I am not this panic.

Often, I'd believe myself, other times I wouldn't, but I kept reminding myself… "I am not my fear; I am not this panic."

Thank you Peyush ma'am

—Max

10

The Magic Of Your Breath

Have you ever felt that life could be scary? That everything is so uncertain?

Uncertainty of unexpected outcomes can cause a feeling of fear and anxiety.

A few years ago, I was caught by phobia. I became a prisoner to it. It choked me so badly that I was forced to learn meditation, yoga, and relaxation techniques. I learned to transform my negative energy into positive, which as a result, changed my thought process from negative waste to positive. The transformation has helped me in a living a positive and happy life.

After a lot of experimentation to overcome this phobia, the easiest and most valuable trick that I learnt was of 'simple breathing technique'. With a five-step breath in and breathe out technique, I am able to calm myself, stop any unfavourable experience to affect me, and reset my day anytime. I was so amazed by its outcome that I could not stop myself from teaching this technique to my friends. It started working very well for each one of them.

With this, I learnt that when people feel restless and agitated, they take hollow and agile breath. This leads to many unfavourable physical symptoms and builds up on anxiety, impatience, etc. Since ancient times, deep breath has been used as a very popular and effective tool to pull oneself out from panic attacks and anxiety.

How does DEEP BREATH work?

Deep breathing is good for physical as well as mental health. Breathing exercises lower your heart rate and soothes your nerves. It has been proved that repeated deep breaths or focusing on breath with closed eyes works wonders in helping a person arrive at a calm and relaxed state of mind. Practicing deep and long breaths can also cure acute states of anxiety and asthma.

A great psychiatrist and founder of Gestalt therapy, Fritz Perls, MD, said; 'Fear is excitement without the breath', which means- the mechanisms that produce excitement also produce fear. Any type of fear can be transformed from fear to excitement by using breathing exercises. Likewise, excitement can be converted into fear when the breath is kept on hold.

As fear and excitement is nothing, but just flow of energy, so the energy can be transformed or converted from one form to another.

Most often, we deny or ignore the threat posed by fear as we think that it will help us to overcome the problem. But it doesn't work this way as Dr. Perls said, "the less breath you feed your fear, the bigger your fear gets."

Fritz Perls, MD, said; "Breathing is exhaling. Most of us commit a mistake when we think breathing is about inhaling. But breathing in true sense is throwing out the bad air." First, we exhale carbon dioxide (CO_2) and then we inhale oxygen in the form of fresh air.

My rendezvous with deep breath

The best advice that I have ever got to face my fear is: "take big, easy breaths when you feel fear. Feel the fear instead of pretending it's not there."

Blow your fear like you blow the candles just before cutting the cake so that you can celebrate the excitement later just like you celebrate once the candles are blown. Repeat the process of breathing as many times as possible for you in a day to make yourself feel calm and excited.

When I practiced the breathing technique, it left me speechless. I was surprised to experience how just a few deep breaths and exhalations can help my brain relax. I was curious to know how it brought so much peace and joy to the soul. How could this long deep breathing process push away all the negative energy of fear and anxiety? As I made deep breath a daily practice, my mind started filling with a million questions. My curiosity warranted me to research further, through which I found some interesting facts related to breath.

Many of us know that our body has a second brain in the stomach, in our gut or alimentary canal, which contains some 100 million neurons. These are more neurons than those present in our spinal cord or the peripheral nervous system. Hence, a big part of our emotions are probably influenced by the nerves in our gut. The popular saying 'butterflies in the stomach' also points out to this fact and is a result of the presence of Serotonin, also called 'happy chemical, which is found in our bowel area. It indicates that our gut is a part of our physiological stress response.

Traditional Chinese medicine has also recognized stomach as the focal point of the human energy system, and has emphasized on finding this centre to restore energy and health.

So, next time, if you or anyone experiences a panic attack, it is best to use deep breathing technique for instant relaxation, and a calming effect.

Breathing is nature's unlimited free gift for which you don't have to pay anything. It is the quickest self-help therapy to eliminate fear and anxiety. So, breathe freely and enjoy its calmness.

11

Gratitude: A Powerful Attitude

Fear or gratitude?

What will you choose? I choose gratitude!

Gratitude is derived from the Latin word "gratia" which means gratefulness and thankfulness. In simple words, gratitude means a 'state of thankfulness' or a 'state of being grateful'.

Everyone wants a happy life, a comfortable job, lovable family, financial independence, and a respectful social life. In this vague quest of happiness and peace, when was the last time when you spared a minute to thank the Universe for what you already have in life?

In this stress-filled life, we have completely forgotten that the things that we have are exactly the same things that a million others are struggling for. Still, we are not thankful!

I started a daily gratitude practice back in 2007. I was in the middle of a major transition in my life and things were hard. Fear used to be my constant companion and I often felt like

I was drowning. Developing a gratitude practice didn't change my circumstances but it did shift my perspective. My fears didn't disappear but practicing gratitude eventually became an important tool for helping me to manage my fears. Since then, I have made gratitude a part of my lifestyle. So much so that when I am eating, I thank Mother Nature, the farmer who raised crops for me and the Almighty who made it possible for me to gather enough resources to put food on the table.

While practicing it in my daily life, I realized that gratitude, in any form, can enlighten our mind and make us feel blissful. So, I store all the grateful events that I have experienced in my life in my bucket of gratitude, and can pick them up whenever I am feeling afraid.

In my experience, we can feel both fear and gratitude together. I know that the two emotions are different poles. They are like the two sides of the sea that can never meet. Each one is of a completely different energy and frequency. Yet, they can occur together.

If you are in gratitude, deep down from the bottom of your heart, the kind of feeling that you have when you experience it right in the core, you will eventually feel fear.

Sounds unbelievable? Give it a shot.

Why choose gratitude?

Every action has an equal and opposite reaction; says Newton's third law. Likewise, if we are more grateful for the existing things in our life, we will attract more things to be grateful for. Gratitude helps us in being optimistic, the end result of which is happiness and joy in life. Expressing gratitude is the road to building strong relationships, helps us to deal better with adverse situations, and enables us to bounce back with a greater strength and determination.

Fear and anxiety can make us feel disempowered. When bereaved of power, we tend to dance on the bare lyrics of anger instead of gratitude. Anger puts off the lights of hope in our life. It pulls us down and gives birth to stress, which gives birth to fear. And, fear makes us a prisoner and shortens our lifespan.

Gratitude, on the other end, is the antidote for fear. Thanksgiving pushes us upward. While fear takes our focus towards our problems, gratitude takes our focus towards the solutions. Gratitude connects us with the supreme power of the Universe. Being in gratitude gives us the feeling of being blessed, irrespective of our situation.

Gratitude attracts happiness in life

There is a multi-dimensional connection between gratitude and happiness. Confessing gratitude to others, and to self induces positive emotions within, essentially happiness. It improves our relationship with others at home and at workplace. It helps us in experiencing solitude and contentment. Not just emotional health, gratitude works wonders for our overall health.

Gratitude is good for health

Every disease in our body is a result of negative emotions stuck within our physical bodies. Gratitude, though, is a natural power of the Universe that brings mental peace to us and keeps us enthusiastic about life. As we practice gratitude and attain mental peace, our physical health also improves.

Gratitude makes you professionally committed

Many egoistic employees believe that they are indispensable for their organization. Similarly, many egoistic owners believe that their employees are only able to earn because of them. Both believe that their contribution to the others life is unmatched, and hadn't it been for them, the other wouldn't have been able to earn or run the organization.

Wouldn't it be wonderful if we could reverse their thoughts! If they could think that "I would never have been able to do it alone. It's so wonderful to have him with me".

This feeling of gratitude can be extremely powerful in improving relationships at workplace and building trust amongst people. It also makes a person more compassionate, considerate, empathetic, and caring towards his colleagues.

Gratitude builds professional commitment

Expressing gratitude at workplace builds interpersonal bonds and triggers feelings of closeness and bonding (Algoe, 2012). Grateful workers are more efficient, more productive, and more responsible.

Employees who practice expressing gratitude at work are more likely to volunteer for more assignments, are willing to take an extra step to accomplish their tasks, and work happily as a part of the team. Also, managers and supervisors who feel grateful and remember to convey the same, have a stronger group cohesiveness and better productivity. They recognize good work, give everyone their due importance in the group, and active communication on with their the team members.

Gratitude overcomes fears

Here are 5 ways that I have learned and experienced about how gratitude helps us to overcome fear.

(a) Gratitude keeps you hopeful

One of the positive side effects of practicing gratitude is that it has kept my hope alive. And hope is one of the most challenging things to hold on to in a worst-case scenario. Gratitude helps to keep hope alive as it shifts our focus from negative to positive, and heaviness to lightness.

All of us have heard – 'what you focus on grows.' Likewise, when you focus more on practicing gratitude, you can emerge more positive and kindle the light of hope within yourself.

(b) Gratitude helps you forget bad experiences

"Forgive and forget" is a very common phrase. But very few are actually successful in practicing this in reality. It is very difficult to forget old sores and bad experiences that might have created fear and stress in our lives. Similarly, it is very difficult for an individual to forgive himself for some unwarranted action in the past. Gratitude helps in either of the cases—be it to overcome the fear of past experiences which never seem to leave you, or to get past the fear of the future.

(c) Gratitude releases pain and toxic emotions

A study conducted on individuals seeking mental health guidance shared a report in which the participants were divided into two groups. One group was asked to write a letter of gratitude while the other group was asked to pen down their negative experiences. Later, it was found that the participants who wrote the letter of gratitude were feeling better and positive, while the participants who wrote their negative experiences felt anxious and stressed.

During another study that was conducted to evaluate the effect of gratitude on physical well-being, it was found that 16% people, who maintained a journal for gratitude, noticed a gradual reduction in their pain. This was since being in gratitude increases their level of Dopamine, a hormone that is responsible for happiness.

(d) Gratitude opens the door of self-imposed prison

A fearful person loves to lock himself in a dark room. Instead, a person who practices gratitude is more open to life. He has faith in self and the Universe. He finds good meaning in life and lives a better life.

(e) Gratitude tranquilizes stress

Gratitude is a natural medicine given by nature to humans to tranquilize their stress. It gives relief to the soul and body. Serenity becomes your original nature when you practice gratitude.

If you choose to practice gratitude over fear, you are courageous. Your choice is ultimate. Make gratitude a part of the lifestyle.

Now that we have spoken about the benefits of gratitude, let us understand the rules of practicing it in reality.

The rules for practicing gratitude

Gratitude requires submission—100 percent submission of your patience. You need to have patience for 90 days to bring this practice into your habit, and a year to build it in your character and make it your lifestyle.

Initially, you might have to do this intentionally and it might make you feel a bit uneasy; especially for people who are very practical in life and may think "how can I be grateful when the reality is dark?" But do not forget: 'every action has an equal and opposite reaction.' So, when you are grateful, you progress. If you celebrate life, life will give you more chances to celebrate in the future.

Everything comes with a mindset in life. Likewise, gratitude— An attitude of gratitude leads our life towards freedom, and allows fear to move past us.

Process of incorporating a gratitude practice

- Be humble
- Accept yourself and others
- Let go of your bad experiences
- Choose happiness

Let's Build a Habit Around Gratitude

Write down two things you're grateful for every day for the next ninety days. Every day, when you wake up, smile, and let the first thought be of 'THANKFULNESS'. Repeat the same thing when you are about to sleep. Do not forget to express your feelings of gratitude to your family, friends, colleagues, and anyone you are grateful to, even your pet. Once you start practicing the habit of gratitude, you will start finding the negative emotions being replaced by positive ones and a sense of mental calm.

Gratitude can be helpful in combating insomnia, substance abuse, and eating disorders, which will automatically reflect in your physical health and help in reducing cardiac diseases, inflammations, and neurodegeneration significantly. People around you will also feel empowered and get inspired by your attitude of gratitude.

Always remember—it is always about attitude. Build an attitude of gratitude.

12

Choose To Surrender

Our life's velocity depends on the motion of our belief system.

We know that fear is the opposite of faith. The reason being, fear is a negative emotion, and faith is a positive emotion. Fear builds a negative belief system and faith builds a positive belief system. And, our entire life's velocity depends on the motion of our belief system.

What motion do you choose? I choose faith.

It allows me to just trust the process. Choosing faith helped me to realize that things become smooth when I trust the process, allowing things to happen instead of making them happen. Hence, when I give up on controlling things and situations, I remain calm and peaceful. Things work better in that state of mind.

This quote by Steve Maraboli has inspired me and reminded me, again and again, to let it go—"You must learn to let go.

Release the stress. You were never in control anyway."

Though it took me a lot of time to bring the habit of 'trusting the process' into practice and make it a lifestyle, I couldn't stop sharing its benefits with people after experiencing them in my life.

The control freak

Once, a lady visited me to be healed. She used to get distressed at very small things in life. If she did not plan things, could not predict them, or control them.

She, once expressed, the questions that come to her mind while planning a trip—"Will my baby sleep well if I am not around? How cranky will she be? What is her sleeping pattern? Can I adjust my travel plans to accommodate that?"

She literally wanted to control everything in and around her. She told me about the several trips that she had cancelled in the past because of her need to predict and control. She also explained how she kept thinking about the weather and its predictions whenever someone was about to visit them from another city, and how she spent all her productive time in planning for every possible weather/mood combination when considering her itinerary. She also spent a lot of time on things that should have otherwise not mattered to her.

With a first-hand experience of working with a person who is obsessed about 'control' and helping her recover, I can share two things:

(a) Fear of "what will happen if we don't"

The majority of people live in fear of "what will happen if we don't control things", a reason why our parents tried to control us right since childhood. The fear must have been passed to them by their parents and so on.

So, how exactly did they control us? They did it by creating fear in our brains.

They said "study hard, else you will fail". What if they could say "study hard so that you score well." Wouldn't it be so much better?

We have been raised in an environment where fear preceded everything else. Our mind got programmed accordingly. Later fear became an existential reality, a part of our lifestyle, and we, just like our parents, started believing that 'control is rooted in fear'.

(b) Fear of "what if I don't get the desired outcome"

Many people are very obsessed with the outcome of the karma they perform. Control is the result of being attached to a specific outcome.

Everyone talks about 'Don't expect the fruits. Just do your deeds.' But how many of us have actually been able to implement this in our life? If we can start practicing this, we will not remain attached to a specific outcome—an outcome we are sure is the best for us (as if we always know what is best).

It becomes easier to let go of things when we trust that things will be fine, no matter what comes our way. The act of just doing your karma without being attached to a specific outcome opens up many more possibilities.

The energy of surrender has more force than to the energy of control

You may have experienced that when we try to control the situation, our mind experiences heavy fluctuation. When we try to control, our mind is filled with a million thoughts which travel at a supersonic speed. Rather than being in the present, our mind travels to the future. This increases the heart rate, shallows our breath and pumps Adrenaline into our body. Alongside, our vision gets slender, our concentration gets adversely affected, memory gets poor, and we lose track of time. Thus, we are unable to make use of the current opportunities.

Instead, when we practice surrendering, we remain peaceful and happy without any reason. Our intellect works with excellence and we are able to perform with 100% accuracy. We become optimistic, which broadens our horizon to see things in life. We remain light and spread light.

The miracle happens when we surrender

Surrender is when you stop trying to control things; stop challenging, fighting, and complaining to self and the Universe; stop resisting reality.

Surrender means trusting the natural flow and process of the Universe.

Surrender = Acceptance + Faith

Acceptance in every situation, faith in every circumstance, without doubting for a moment and without giving any input.

I am not saying that you should not perform your karma or get into the action zone. No!

Remind yourself of what is written in Bhagwat Geeta- 'Don't expect the fruits. Just do your deeds'. Perform your karma and take actions but from the place of surrendering to the energy of the Universe and Almighty (whichever supernatural power you believe in).

Initially, you will have to shift your mind very deliberately and consciously, from control to surrender. And choose to let go.

It was not easy for me when I started. But, slowly, as I paid more attention, I came into higher awareness. To ease things, I used to imagine that I was in a small boat, paddling upstream, against the current. It used to be hard. It used to be a fight. But, once it became a habit, my focus changed and I started to visualize that the boat was turning around, I was dropping the oars and floating downstream. I felt as if I am being pulled to the shore, very gently, without any efforts on my part. Today, simply breathing and saying, "Let go of the oars" is usually enough to get me there.

When you decide to begin and shift from control to surrender, here are a few questions that you can ask yourself. Answers to these will help you to shift your focus:

(a) What am I scared of? What do I think will happen if I let go of the control?

Whenever you spot the fear, question its gravity. Ask yourself, 'is it genuine or an illusion?' If you're scared that the night will be ravaged if your husband doesn't remember to pick up the eggplant (and you have already reminded him fifteen times), question your prediction.

Could you really know the night would be ravaged without the eggplant? And, if it would be ravaged (according to your prediction, anyway), what is so bad about it? Could you really do anything about it?

(b) Whose business am I in – mine or someone else's?

Ask yourself- "Is it really my business or am I poking my nose into someone else's business?" Whenever you are in someone else's business, you are bound to feel uncomfortable.

Before you even attempt to mind someone else's business and put your feet into his shoes, it is essential that you have an idea of his shoe size and if they are compatible with your feet. Think, how is it going to be helpful to get into someone else's shoes?

(c) Does letting go feel like freedom?

Probe what letting go will feel like. Think– "If I can choose sadness, why can't I choose freedom?"

You are free to choose anything. Then choose positivity and good energy for yourself. Let the feeling of freedom be your tool that can guide you towards loosening your hook.

The friendly Universe

Our brain, by natural design, is engineered to predict, control, define, and protect us from threats. Thus, we try to create an environment that can help us to live in safety. We prevent things that might stimulate fear. We keep thinking about the uncertainties, and unpredictability of life. We resist change and feel uneasy about it. As thoughts flow and we try to fight and control everything, life feels like a burden. We start regretting the bad experiences and failures in our past. We start predicting the future. As a result, we are unable to savour the blessings of the present moment, of being alive! And, slowly, fear infringes our happiness and peace.

What we do not know is that everything that is happening in this Universe is for good. Every change is for our growth. Change is the law of nature. Everything changes—the season and our body; the earth moves and shifts; life constantly changes and presents new challenges. And, in everything that changes, good things occur. Unaware of the goodness that comes from this change, we fear it and try to control it.

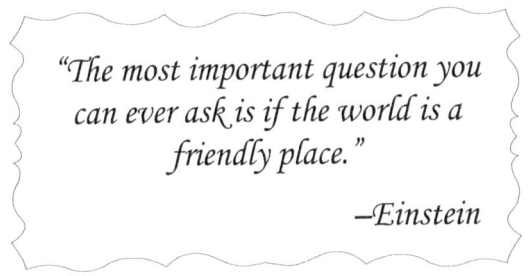

"The most important question you can ever ask is if the world is a friendly place."

—Einstein

I believe in what Einstein said- A friendly Universe.

Try to believe that the Universe is a friendly place. Trust in the process of the goodness of life. Accept that challenges aren't bad but are opportunities to grow. Accept change as it comes. Accept that life is not in our control, and that it is constantly changing. Change is its nature and it is changing for our benefit.

Acknowledge your fear, allow it to flow and release. Let it go. Accept the feelings of anxiety, frustration, anger, fear, jealousy, and embarrassment, or any other negative emotion just as you accept your fever or any other physical pain in your body. Treat these negative emotions as you treat the physical pain. When you experience fear, notice the thought patterns in your mind. Witness the inner experience as energy passes through your heart. Relax your shoulders and your belly. Stay alert and receptive to identify the cause of tension in your body and mind. Don't get over-possessive while observing this process. Just relax and allow the sensation to flow. Then, breathe deeply and allow distress to dissipate and move through you. Just observe it as energy and let it go.

Let's not block ourselves from experiencing absolute joy by living half-heartedly. Isn't that unfair to ourselves? Allow fear to move through you. Be willing to open up, and accept anything and everything that comes your way. Doing this will help you to rise up with courage and determination, and you will be able to do what you really want to do.

The Universe needs your creative and unique prowess. Don't allow your fear to pull you down. Embrace the process of the Universe and celebrate life.

13

Beyond Genetics

*M*y counselee, Nisha, once confided in me about one of her deepest fears. She was afraid that her husband might fall very sick one day. This fear was based on the fact that her mother- in-law, who was a cancer patient, must have passed on her cancer- causing genes to his son, Nisha's husband. Then, we discussed Epigenetics and she was extremely surprised and relieved to know that our genetic structure can be changed with the power of our thoughts and environment, and that working upon these aspects can certainly help her husband turn the harmful genes off within his body.

We know how our genetic structure significantly impacts our body and defines various traits and characteristics. Since long we believed that we are the result of our genes; that our characteristics, physical attributes and health have been passed on by our ancestors. We thought that there was nothing that could really be done about how our genes react and respond within us.

This loss of control causes enormous fears amongst. We always live in the fear of inheriting our parental genes and thus their diseases and abnormalities. A person with a family history of bad genes is always worried about being diagnosed with some genetic problems, thanks to the transmission of genes!

Though, Epigenetics proves it otherwise.

What is Epigenetics?

Epigenetics is the study of the additional factors, over and above our traditional genetic inheritance, that turn our genes on and off, in turn impacting how our cells read and communicate with them. These additional factors may be our environment, lifestyle, diet, external factors or various other physiological traits.

The science of Epigenetics explains that our DNA alone does not control our biology. It says that our genetic structure can be altered and reprogrammed by using the power of our mind, which includes our thoughts, beliefs and perceptions. Changing these, in combination with other external elements, can trigger various epigenetic changes, which can further change how our DNA is decoded by our cells, either boosting or blocking the transcription. Reprogramming our genetic structure then leads to visible changes in related traits and characteristics.

Consider a movie where your DNA is the scriptwriter and the cells are your actors and actresses. The DNA has written every sequence that is supposed to be enacted in the movie. Now, Epigenetics—the director steps in. He decides certain sequences to be of no good and eliminates them, and gives a new direction to the whole screenplay. He decides which original parts or genes would find expression and which would not, thus deciding the course of the movie; just like Epigenetics decides the course of everything that we experience in life.

Epigenetics can battle our fears

Most often we blame our health problems on our genes. Those

with a family history of diabetes, heart problem, hypertension, cancer and various other diseases find it easier to state them as reasons for their poor health. Believing that we are prone to bad health just because we have it in our genes leads us to a victim mentality and we feel disempowered.

But now we know that having a bad gene does not mean that it has to work similarly on us as it did for our parents or their parents. We do have the power to change our genetic expression, and deactivate the unfavourable genes or activate the favourable ones. Dr. Bruce Lipton, a cell biologist, researcher, and the author of the bestseller 'The Biology of Belief, Bruce Lipton', introduced the  modern science of Epigenetics to the world. While applying the principles of quantum physics to his research, he studied the impact of the external environment on the cell's behaviour and noticed that our nutrition, stress, emotions and thoughts are the key contributors in changing the cell's physiology, and thus its ability to read our genes. Of these factors, the subtle energy that emerges from our negative and positive thoughts, beliefs and perceptions are the ones that make the strongest difference in gene modification.

The study proved that once we can identify the self-limiting thoughts and other factors that are responsible for activating or deactivating the genetic transcription, we can send out different information to our cells by changing them. This change in information to our cells leads our cells to respond, and communicate differently with our genes. In this way, we can create a significant difference in our health and other aspects and live a happier and carefree life, irrespective of our genes that makes Epigenetics a true warrior in our battle against fear of genes.

Key Highlights

- We can take complete control of our genes and turn them on or off
- Our thoughts have the strongest impact on genetic expression
- We can change our genetic structure by changing the external environment
- We can be healthy and happy irrespective our inherited genetic structure

How epigenetics works?

Our DNA or genetic structure sits at the middle of every cell, the nucleus. The genes in our DNA are constantly interacting with its cell, triggering it to form the necessary proteins which are essential to conduct various biological actions and enable our life functions. Epigenetic changes can interfere with the ability of our cells to read these genes by turning them on or off with help of some chemical tags. These chemical tags are defined by the communication between our cells, and the external environment which includes our thoughts, beliefs, perceptions, diet, lifestyle and various other factors. If the genes become silent, it restricts the production of the relevant proteins within the cell. On the other hand, if the epigenetic changes make the genes easier to be transcribed, it enhances the production of relevant proteins within the cell. This in turn, will decide how our bodies behave in response to our existing genetic structure and the changes induced through epigenetics.

(a) The power that we hold within

Epigenetics has proved that our thoughts, consciousness, perceptions and lifestyle have an immense impact on our genetic restructuring. By restructuring these key elements, something that we have full control on, we can exercise our power on our genes, and take complete charge of our health and life.

(b) Power of thought

With every thought that we have, we release chemicals into our body. So, by merely changing a single thought, we can change the chemicals being released into our body, in turn causing epigenetic changes, changing how our genes are communicating with our cells. Now, imagine what can happen if we focus our thoughts to something that we really desire. It would have a cascading effect on our genes and subsequently our health.

This means that we are the master of our genes. That is the kind of life-changing power that we hold within. Just by changing what we are thinking right now, at this very moment, we can change how our genes respond within our bodies, and avoid all the harmful effects that it can have on our body and mind.

(c) Power of perception

We are surrounded by a multitude of information and data. But how we perceive this information and interpret it all makes the difference. The meaning that we attach to our environment and our reality, triggers various chemicals within our cells and drives subsequent biological changes. These perceptions continuously affect our neural structures and impact, who we are on a broad level as well as on our genetic levels. Over time, these changes cause our genes to switch on or off.

So, how we perceive a situation, environment or information can go a long way in making our genes respond in a certain way, leading us to avoid or go through various genetic diseases. A mere change in our perception can be very empowering, and create an enormous change in the quality of our life.

(d) Power of consciousness

As human beings, we have the ability to lead a conscious life and make conscious choices about who we are, how we think and respond, what we believe and the life we live. The power of consciousness that we hold within is very empowering when it comes to genetic reengineering. Epigenetics explains how human consciousness plays a vital role in our gene expression, and helps us to stay healthier.

One of the most effective ways of unleashing the power of consciousness is to meditate. Meditation calms the body and mind, and releases favourable chemicals inside our cells, in turn attracting favourable gene response.

(e) Power of Lifestyle

Our lifestyle choices which include what we eat, our physical routine, sleeping patterns, stress levels, exposure to contaminants, the environment we live in, our relationships, and everything else can influence how our genes respond within our bodies, and may deteriorate or improve health.

It has been proved that lifestyle-induced epigenetic changes keep happening throughout life and are reversible. For instance, exposure to excessive pollution can alter the chemical tag in our DNA, and increase the chances for neurodegenerative disease. On the flip side, rich intake of Vitamin C may protect our body from the harmful effects of pollution and reduce our risk of becoming unhealthy. Keeping a close watch on these and leading an affirmative life can be extremely rewarding when it comes to genetic restructuring, and a great health.

Considering all the above factors, the science of epigenetics can certainly be called a healing revolution and if studied well and used as a positive tool, it has the ability to turn around your genetic structure, and make your health and life like you can never imagine.

So, do away with all your fears and explore how to bring epigenetics into real use.

14

Key Takeaways

A little fear can be healthy. But more of it can stop you from living your life to the fullest.

I understand that feeling of being afraid to begin the process to overcome your fear. I know how fearful that feels. However, there is only one thing worse than a quitter—a person who never began.

Dale Carnegie once said: "Inaction breeds doubt and fear. Action breeds confidence and courage. If you would like to overcome fear, don't sit in reception and believe it. Go out and get busy."

Don't let fear block your success. If you truly want to find ways to regulate your fear and rise in your life and career, I have some amazing ideas that have worked for me. They can work for you too.

- Explore your memories. Look back at your life. Question, "What situations gave birth to my fears?" Do you see any common denominators? When was the last time you were afraid to do something and did it away?

- Look at your responsibilities. You have a lot of priorities in your life. Which ones make you fearful? Why are you afraid of them? Dig deep, and keep asking "why" until you are satisfied that you have found the root of your fear.

- Construct a worst-case scenario. When a particular situation makes you nervous, try considering the worst thing that the situation could realistically lead to. Chances are that the reality will not be as devastating as you think, and examining the possibilities ahead of time will prepare you for the potential pitfalls.

- Shift your focus. When you are confronted by a task that makes you fearful, stop, and think about all the positive benefits it will produce in the end. Focusing on the result helps you to set the tiny worries aside.

- Try new things. At every opportunity, plan a replacement task or a special responsibility. This will increase your capacity to take risks. It will also expand your skill set and build your confidence.

- Review your risks. Look at some of the risks that you have taken recently. Chances are that most of them turned out to be alright. Figure out what made them work. Can you duplicate those decisions that led to past success and apply them to other situations?

- Know that your fear will resurface occasionally. Accept this fact because there will be times when you will still be out of control, and the external factors might influence the situation adversely. Prepare yourself to handle disappointments. Stop and assess the circumstances so that you get to know if further actions will help or hurt.

- Always be in a surrendering mode. Believe that whatever is happening is happening for your good. The more you accept this, the easier your life will be. If you don't accept it, you will find it difficult to live.

- Live in this moment. Live happily as if this is the last moment of your life. Love yourself to overcome your fear. Spread love between people.

- Pay gratitude. Be grateful from morning till the time you go to bed. Make gratitude like your second breath. The more gratitude you pay, more opportunities will be created by the Universe to be grateful for.

- Work on your belief system. Change it in your favour. Break your thresholds.

Now knowing how to control your fear can have disastrous results. Take action. Master this emotion. Be in complete control of your life and live in complete blissfulness and abundance.

Quiz Time

After teaching my readers almost everything about Fear that is worth knowing, I want to make you all immune to this menace.

No matter, whether you have mild symptoms of getting engulfed with fear, or you are asymptomatic, just Take this Fear Quiz and send your answers at the address given below:

_____

_____

_____

The hologram of this book will be the entry pass of this test.

You will not need to pay money once you show the hologram. This precious gift will be available to my readers only. Rest assured, whether Fear is new entrant in your mind, or it is Chronic, you will be able to do away with this for sure.

Writing the Book Alone on this subject was never my dream

My dream was to make you immune to this success-obstructing, depressing, life intimidating emotion.

Come and Join me to Drive Fear out of your Mind!!

You can connect with me at:

✉ journeywithin.co.in

🌐 peyushbhatia.com

f peyushbhatialifecoach

📷 peyushbhatialifecoach/

in peyush-bhatia-670abb86/